W9-DAA-983

S UNDER 20
WMale, age 21, 5'5", Bl hair grn eyes,
quiet, speak Polish, some English, +
t dominate sadistic age 12 to ?? for
iend etc. No heavy S&M relationship
ted, just light discipline & humilation!
so want to exchange ex
ple who like hoys una

IF YOU'RE YOUNG,
im, not on drugs, no weirdo and would
the finer things; from love to yach
avel, if you're tired of knoc
uld like a mature man (4
you can give of yourse
xury living without being
en I'd like to meet you. All
clude recent photo and pho

SMOOTH INNOC
Ext goodlooking athle
desired. Your place.

**2 SKATEBOARD
SURFERS**
2 super chickens off the side
walk & in your home, ready to

for you. Take your pick of everything
from springers to roosters. Details sent
following dtld letter from you. Box

**YOUNG & VERY ATTR
BLOND BLUE EYED MODEL
AT YOUR PLACE OR MINE
5'7", 130 LBS
SMOOTH BODY SWIMMERS
LL ANYTIME
UP BOYS**
dults only! Fully
e to go, what to
Mail.
age.

nteresting.
ree catalog

## Like 'er
A quarter brings deta
ones in mind. Ten
gossip sheet. C.C. C

AMAJCA
ay Male- Age 1
thers around m
ossible- Be di

**LEAN LONG**
wanted by hairy, bald
a friend, model, or ? (

**WANTED YOU**
Love poss w/strong, sinc
old int'l businessma
bodybuilder w/sophistica
town San Francisco see
muscular youth for on goi
ship
Fra        **WANTED Y**
happ Live-in poss w/s
Int'l businessman
bldr w/sophistic

LINOIS
Male, 20's, ru
eeds many teen
oom & board +
ummer months.
esume and pict

**LOST AND LON**
u are very young, slim, wi
aid to face life alone, wi
ve; you need a tall, hairy,
e and protect you and live
d take care of him. Send

**CHICKEN**
Chicken lover with
from others. JOHN

**GAY BOYS: LIKE TRAV**
Wealthy w/m 32, lookin
treactive well-built w/stu
for sex, travel, fun.

F YOU WANT THE VERY BEST
TREAT YOURSELF TO A
CALIFORNIA GOLDEN BOY!

king. The captain
d beats him with
n pain each time
ass, leaving red
! The handsome,
e cadet get it on
m, $26. 7-5x7s, $7;
order. Fast ser-

Youth
from young sur-
S.F. Bay Area?
ular visits from
tin o.k. (415) 929-

I'm blond
. Want to
age, also
etc. Pic
D!
homes until
ok off, and
en. I turned
Moon Child
hair almost
by ok the
eems empty
cares. If you
reciate it. If
ollars to help
e great. But
nd send you
519 Gar-

got 'em prin-
have two
among your
g: NEEKID
each or both
re on young
ome cinema.
es sweet,
dly, under
nd cut.
or drugs.

Bi- WMale- Age 28- Very generous- desires
WMale under 17- Prefer experienced for friendship etc. Will travel. Please send pic.

# For Money or Love ♂

# For Money or Love:

## Boy Prostitution in America

*by*

# Robin Lloyd

*With an Introduction by*
*Senator Birch Bayh*

VANGUARD PRESS, INC.
NEW YORK

Copyright © 1976 by Robin Lloyd
Published by Vanguard Press, Inc.
424 Madison Avenue, New York, N.Y. 10017
Published simultaneously in Canada by
Gage Publishing Co., Agincourt, Ontario.
Library of Congress Catalogue Card Number: 75-40691
ISBN: 0-8149-0773-3
Designer: Tom Torre Bevans
Manufactured in the United States of America.

2 3 4 5 6 7 8 9 10

To my son Carlos, who keeps life
warm with the sunshine of his smile.
. . . and to our Bobby who, in November, 1975,
took the ultimate trip . . . without us.

# Table of Contents

# Introduction

by SENATOR BIRCH BAYH *

As Chairman of the Senate Subcommittee to Investigate Juvenile Delinquency, I have spent much of my time exploring the various causes and possible cures for delinquency and criminal behavior in our young people. I have listened to hundreds of witnesses, including juvenile judges, schoolteachers, child psychologists, probation officers, delinquent children and those who might well have become delinquents if they hadn't received the proper guidance. From this evidence emerges a picture of American children in trouble, many of the troubles not caused by the children themselves but by policymakers and others insensitive to their needs.

Robin Lloyd's report is frightening in its accuracy, with much of his data matching that heard by the Subcommittee from other sources. His case histories generated from his own sources are similar to case histories now a matter of Congressional record. While his book deals specifically with a hitherto undiscussed facet of the homosexual world, it primarily deals with juvenile delinquency. Lloyd correctly targets the cause not as a proclivity toward a specific sexual orientation, but as a seemingly general public disinterest in children.

Juvenile delinquency covers a broad area ranging from truancy to capital offenses and, right now, it presents an alarming picture that could get worse. For example, the number of American students who died in the combat zones of our nation's

---

* The Honorable Birch Bayh, Member, U.S. Senate (Dem.-Ind.), Chairman, U.S. Senate Subcommittee to Investigate Juvenile Delinquency

schools between 1970 and 1973 exceeded the number of American soldiers killed in combat in the first three years of the Vietnam War.

As Lloyd mentions, in 1974, a committee of the New York State Legislature revealed that in some New York City high schools, students ran narcotic, firearm and prostitution rings. It is not only a big-city problem. In my own state of Indiana, a ring was discovered in a junior high school that extorted money from forty of the other children! Our recent studies have confirmed that children in trouble defy geographical, economic and cultural boundaries.

The quality of school education is, in many cases, the determining factor in whether a youth becomes a contributing, useful member of society or embarks on a life of frustration and failure, eventually leading to violence and crime. For far too many, education becomes only a lesson in the cruelty of unfulfilled promises. Many youths flee such disappointment or failure. The children who run look for companionship, friendship and approval from those they meet. Many such youths are easy marks for gangs, drug pushers and pimps. Runaways often sell drugs or their bodies, and steal to support themselves. In this way, the runaway incident, as with other noncriminal acts such as truancy, serves as the young person's initial contact with the world of criminal activity. The longer communities ignore such problems, the greater the likelihood that future behavior will be far more serious.

It is important for those concerned with the future of our young people to understand both the gravity of the situation and the obstacles these problems raise for the future of our children. The generation gap is very real. One million young Americans run away from home every year and we have drifted into a condition where many youths are apart from the community instead of being a part of it.

Testimony before the Subcommittee established that these

youngsters need temporary shelter, short-term counseling and other assistance that, it is hoped, will result in a voluntary return to healthy homes. But in spite of the clearly demonstrated need it was not until national attention was focused on the horrifying murders of dozens of runaways in Houston that officials in the Executive Branch tempered their opposition to Congressional efforts to aid these children and their families.

I believe that Lloyd's book will similarly help to arouse our collective conscience, which will in turn lead to policies and behavior more sensitive to children in trouble.

Clearly such dramatic impetuses are necessary, for while the Nixon and Ford Administrations profess to be shocked and concerned over juvenile delinquency, they responded with indifference to Congressional initiative to control the skyrocketing increase in juvenile crime and delinquency. For example, they opposed the bipartisan allocation by Congress of 75 million dollars earmarked to prevent delinquency that costs the nation over 12 billion dollars, year after year.

The problem of juvenile delinquency does not call for the changing of existing social values. It calls for the examination of which are true and meaningful values, and which, through changing conditions, have become meaningless.

I heartily endorse Lloyd's suggestion for a department of youth at a cabinet level. He has done much to demonstrate its necessity.

As we celebrate our two-hundredth birthday as a nation, contributions such as *For Money or Love* will help to assure that our third century will more fully acknowledge that our young people are the Nation's most valuable resource.

I firmly believe that we can and must act in a manner that truly offers our children an open road to the pursuit of happiness, and, as Father McGinness says in this book: "If we don't do it . . . who will?"

# Author's Preface

I was led into this story by my two boys: my son Carlos, then eighteen, and my ward Bobby, fifteen. Both have been brought up in the turbulent world of a reporter, much closer to the harsh realities of life than most boys their age. Whenever possible they go with me on assignments, so they've been exposed to a wide variety of experiences.

They've parachuted out of airplanes, had dinner with Billy Sol Estes, loaded cameras for me in hurricanes, visited prisons, watched electric-shock therapy, and mixed it up with police in civil-rights disturbances. Carlos has been photographed with Senator George McGovern, with a noted Mafia leader, and with the police as they pulled an accident victim—in three pieces—out of a five-car collision. Bobby was arrested along with his friends for protesting the shutdown of a municipal swimming pool, and was responsible for plunging a large section of Los Angeles into darkness after cutting a high-voltage line with a pair of garden shears.

Other than that, they're regular boys. They have confronted a cross section of the problems one encounters when growing up in modern America and they have, along with many other members of their generation, learned the difference between rhetoric and reality. In their spare time they go to dances, work out at the gym, search through record stores, and dream aloud about making movies. Yet, even though they have not led sheltered lives, are not too unusual, and are able to handle most situations, they let themselves become involved in an episode for which they were not prepared.

During their 1973 summer vacation, when they came home one afternoon, supposedly from the beach, I knew something out of the ordinary had happened: I recognized their sidelong glances as an indication they had been involved in some sort of joint enterprise. Carlos picked up the cue from Bobby and said, almost too casually, "We had our pictures taken today for a magazine."

"Oh?" I said. "What magazine?"

"We don't know the name. This guy came up to us and said he wanted to take a series of pictures of what two boys do during vacation on a hot summer's day."

I sat down. "How did you meet him?"

Bobby replied, "We were waiting for the bus to go to the beach and he came up and asked if we'd pose for him."

There was something about the word 'pose' I didn't like. "What do you mean 'pose'? Where did you go with him?"

It was Carlos's turn again. "First he photographed us while we were waiting for the bus; then we went down to Stoner Park and he took some more pictures."

There was a brief period of silence, so I prompted, "Then what?"

Bobby said uncomfortably, "We went to his house . . ."

Right then I knew what had happened! The time for parrying was over. I said grimly, "Are you going to tell me he wanted you to pose in the nude?"

Bobby mumbled, "Well . . . sort of."

I snapped, "What the hell is sort-of-nude? You took your clothes off or you didn't."

Carlos hurriedly jumped in with, "Well, we did, but there wasn't any sex stuff. I mean he didn't try to score with us or make any suggestions like that or anything."

I sarcastically said, "Just two typical naked boys in a stranger's house on a hot sumer day . . . ?"

Bobby protested, "Hey, don't worry about it! We have his

name, his address, and his phone number. Besides, Carlos took down his license-plate number in case it wasn't his house."

Somewhat mollified, I delivered a blistering lecture on dumbness, on knowing better, on what things like that could lead to; and I included an opinion on the condition of their rooms.

My first thought was they had met a working pornographer not a photographer. I immediately inquired about the man through friends of mine at the Los Angeles Police Department. They were unaware of my sons' acquaintance. I then called the photographer and made arrangements for a meeting.

What happened when I confronted him, and how the matter was resolved, will go unrecorded except for one detail of lasting importance: when I looked at the prints and the negatives that had been given to me, I saw pictures not only of my sons but also of three other boys. I'd never seen them before and neither had my sons. They, and the photographer's full-time job as an assistant football coach at a fashionable high school, made me wonder how many others had posed for him.

A few days later, during a telephone conversation with a reporter in Washington, D.C., I mentioned the incident. My friend cautioned, "You might have fallen on the fringe area of a very big business. Some of the newspapers here have been running stories about boys being lured into that sort of thing in New York."

He forwarded to me copies of articles that described an increasingly successful business involving adult males and young boy prostitutes. Through the facilities of NBC NEWS in Los Angeles, where I was working, I started to check with other stations across the country to see whether there were similar activities going on in their backyards. The responses were positive.

That happened in July, 1973.

One month later the story of the Houston mass murders broke: law-enforcement officers dug up the bodies of twenty-seven young boys who had been tortured and murdered by three homosexual psychopaths.

In September, 1973, police in Dallas discovered a call-boy ring that offered its members a catalog of young boys seeking "sponsors." The sponsors paid an annual membership fee for the catalog, which listed the names of thousands of young males.

In October, 1973, the Los Angeles police arrested two men for selling movies of young boys engaged in homosexual acts. Subsequently, a full-scale investigation was launched to determine whether there was any connection with the Houston murders. In November the Los Angeles police charged fourteen adults with a total of ninety crimes against a group of boys who were all under thirteen years of age. The charges involved the molestation of children and the production of pornographic books and movies. The youngest of the boys involved was six years old. There was, however, no evidence to link this group to the Houston murders.

During the same month police in Union City, New Jersey, raided a downtown hotel room. They found eight near-naked boys whose average age was twelve. Three adults were arrested for prostituting children.

Meanwhile, citizens of San Antonio, Texas, were shocked to read that a grand jury had reported boy prostitution was big business in their city and that the action was possibly under syndicate control.

It was then that I decided to do the research for this book.

I confronted my two boys with the startling information I'd collected and then asked them—hopefully—if they'd learned anything from it. Their reaction was a reflection of today's teenage mores. Carlos merely shrugged. Bobby said jauntily, "Never take candy from a stranger unless he gives you a ride in his car first!"

Over the past several years, thirteen states have liberalized or decriminalized their sex-act laws. While these changes vary from state to state, they all have one thing in common: any sex act between consenting adults is now usually considered legal, provided the acts are carried out in private and do not infringe on the rights of anyone else. These laws are generally referred to as Consenting Adult Bills.

This book, however, is not so much about consenting adults as about consenting children—specifically young boys. It is not only about the still-misunderstood world of the homosexual but about a sub-rosa culture that spans both the homosexual and heterosexual societies.

Books dealing with sexual mores are comparatively easy to write if you take the popular approach: first state a position, then bolster it with psychiatric evidence proving your point. Whatever position you choose to take, even if it deals with something as exotic as the relationship of bestiality to campanology, there will be a school of psychiatry, or at least an individual with impressive credentials, ready to support your contention. I have not taken this approach. I am not a psychiatrist or a psychologist; neither do I pretend to any amateur status in those august fields. I am an investigative reporter whose area of expertise is getting people to share with me things they would not ordinarily share with anyone, checking and rechecking that information, and then presenting it to the public in a fair, and objective, and understandable manner.

Because of its subject matter, this is not the type of book you will want to send Aunt Matilda for Christmas. It will take you places to which you would not ordinarily go and show you things you would not ordinarily see. This book distills, from the confused brew of modern-day sexuality, a culture that is, in itself, unique; directly, or indirectly, it affects hundreds of thousands of people . . . perhaps you. It is not an uplifting book because, while the subject itself is grim enough, the documented facts make it even grimmer. But, even though it paints a dark picture, it has not been overly dramatized for shock value. You will not find positive solutions to proven problems because of the complexity of the problems themselves. I have, however, offered suggestions on what might be done in the way of a starting point if we really want to begin.

The preparation of *For Love or Money* required a great deal of cooperation from many people who deserve to be acknowledged. To thank each and every one would require a separate book. To those of you not mentioned—either because of an omission on my part or because I was requested not to do so—my many thanks. I have listed others by category, which also serves to indicate the wide variety of input I have received.

DISTRICT ATTORNEYS:

Henry Wade, Dallas; Carol S. Vance, Houston; and a special thanks to Deputy District Attorney James Grodin, Los Angeles.

POLICE OFFICERS:

Capt. Lawrence Hepburn, New York Police Department; Sgt. William McCarthy, New York Police Department; Sgt. Don Smith, Administrative Vice, Los Angeles Police Department; and Sgt. Tom Hensley, Santa Clara, California Police Department; also Clyde Cronkhite, Commander, Juvenile Division, Los Angeles Police Department.

JUVENILE JUDGE:

David Kenyon, Los Angeles.

GAY COMMUNITY LEADERS:

Dr. Bruce Voeller, National Gay Task Force, New York; Morris Kight, Los Angeles.

MINISTERS:

Rev. Troy Perry, Metropolitan Community Church, Los Angeles; Rev. Jack McGinnis, Our Lady of St. John, Houston.

ATTORNEYS:

Steve Bercu, El Paso, Texas; Patrick Keenan, DePaul Law School, Chicago; Peter Sandman, Youth Law Center, San Francisco.

PRESS:

Dewey Gram, *Newsweek*; Leo Janis, *Time*; Doug Sarff, *News West*, Los Angeles; Frank Grenard, WBBM RADIO, Chicago; Bruce MacDonnell, WRC-TV (NBC), Washington, D.C.; Tad Dunbar, KOLO-TV (ABC), Reno, Nevada; Herb Humphries, KMOX-TV (CBS), St. Louis, Missouri; and the helpful library staffs at the *New York Times*, the *Los Angeles Times* and the *Milwaukee Sentinel*.

STATE AND FEDERAL OFFICIALS:

John M. Rector, Staff Director, Senate Sub-Committee to Investigate Juvenile Delinquency; Dr. Jerome Miller, Commissioner of Children and Youth for Pennsylvania; George Saleebey, Deputy Director, California Youth Authority; David Glascock, Assistant Deputy to Ed Edelman, County Supervisor, Los Angeles; and Wayne Kidwell, State Attorney General, Idaho.

NBC, NEW YORK:

Tom Snyder, Pamela Burke, and Joel Tator, all of NBC's "Tomorrow" show.

KNBC NEWS, LOS ANGELES:

There are just too many who helped on a daily basis by keeping their eyes on the wire-machines for me to acknowledge—Terry Gill, Jerry Welzel, Al Kaul, Mike McCormick, John Flynn, and Charlotte Perry among others. Executive Producer Irwin Safchik who kept insisting, "the word is 'among,' not 'amongst,'" and staff-writer Jim Warras, who came up with the title for the book and then whined incessantly until I promised to give him credit for it.

AND TO:

Paul Mace, Johnny Williamson, and Mary Cummings, who handled the typing and provided valuable input. To George Bane, my attorney and friend; to David Hull, my agent, who did much more than any writer has the right to expect; and to Tom Woll, who handled the editing.

But my greatest debt is to the boys themselves. So many of them: troubled, defiant, lost, confused, belligerent, and unhappy.

They're all out there right now, doing God knows what. It's unlikely they'll ever read this book, but, if they do, my deepest thanks.

—R.L.

PART

# I

## THE
## CASE

# 1

# Jimmy
# and the East Coast

*"Never take candy from
a stranger—unless...."*

Boys are selling themselves not only in the cities of New York, Los Angeles, San Francisco, Philadelphia, Chicago, Baltimore, and New Orleans, but also in smaller towns across the country: Waukesha, Wisconsin; Santa Clara, California; Laredo, Texas and in even smaller towns.

In street jargon, the boys are known as "chickens"; their customers as "chickenhawks." In the major cities, young male hookers wander through the streets in search of customers while call-boy operations flourish. Pimps, skilled in initiating young runaways into the highly profitable, low-skill trade, prowl bus depots and other transportation centers, looking for incoming, unattached teen-agers. On occasion, an unwilling boy is transformed into a male prostitute by drugs and brute force; kept as a prisoner until his usefulness has been exhausted.

Most chickens are the sons of working-class or welfare parents, who, because of despair or disinterest, have turned away from their children. For these boys, the lure of easy money, no matter how it is earned, is irresistible. Many have never before performed a homosexual act and do not regard themselves as homosexuals. A surprisingly large minority of the chickens are products of well-to-do but broken families and, in many cases, are attracted to the trade not so much for money as for what they interpret as affection.

After talking to hundreds of these boys in different places and reading hundreds of their case histories from juvenile-bureau files, certain patterns started to take shape; common denominators fell into place. Using these, it was possible to sketch a composite of the boys who come to the big cities looking for a better deal and a better life. Jimmy is typical of this group; so is his introduction to the trade.

He is twelve years old. Small and slender, with an inquisitive expression, he *looks* twelve. His life in a small, depressed town in West Virginia was like that of thousands of his counterparts in similar towns across the country. His father was often unemployed; his mother was a drunken illiterate. A flock of brothers and sisters eliminated any hope of individual attention, except when Jimmy did something wrong, which was often. He had been in and out of juvenile courts for minor offenses, though he had never been committed to a juvenile institution.

Jimmy, like thousands of others, was an unwanted child: the result of a sweaty, grunting, beery, Friday-night wrestling match by his parents. He had never known love, concern, control, guidance, or assistance. Adults were people he lived with. Teachers, who droned on through specified teaching plans, were not interested in either the subjects they taught or the students, who were equally uninterested. Jimmy was failing in school. He couldn't read and really didn't want to. He was told he had a low IQ, though he didn't care much about that. It didn't occur to him that he had done poorly on a recent test because he couldn't read the questions.

His basic knowledge of sex had been picked up from friends in the boys' rest room. Apart from masturbation, his practical sex experience was nil if you discount a frantic, but unsatisfactory, probing attempt with a younger sister.

Jimmy meandered aimlessly through life with no goals, no plans, no future. He had never known hope, excitement, or anticipation. Life to him was a lead-gray sky that poured out a ceaseless, corrosive drizzle of disapproval.

Jimmy's entertainment—and for all practical purposes, his education—came from television. But television taught him about another world. Nobody drove a Maserati in his town. He'd never met a super-cop who would listen to his problems with sympathetic understanding. He couldn't relate to the father on "Rifleman" or "My Three Sons" or to the beautiful lady spraying the $700 carpet with an aerosol spray cleaner. While television tantalized him with the advantages of wealth, power, and love, it didn't show him how to get them.

Although Jimmy's departure from home was brought on by a multiplicity of little things, the climax came when his father, after a hard day of working and an evening of drinking, heard about another bad report card and a neighbor's complaint. Enraged, he beat Jimmy . . . again.

Seeking escape, Jimmy skidded and slipped down the muddy hillside next to his family's dilapidated shack. With tears streaming down his filth-smeared face, he resolved to run away. For the first time in his life, he felt calm and determined.

The next day he learned about excitement and anticipation, discovered purpose, and made decisions. New York City was the place. Jimmy, unaware of work permits, child-labor laws, and social-security cards, believed he would get a job, rent a room, and make his own way. But the first thing to do was get there—and that would take money.

Within a week Jimmy had raised close to forty dollars;

twelve of it by stealing and selling a friend's bike; another seven by going through the pockets of a drunk lying in an alley; and a couple more from the sale of Coke bottles he had collected. Jimmy was still short of money, but on the morning he left a hurried search through his house netted a crumpled five-dollar bill and some change.

After dumping the contents of a small, battered suitcase on the kitchen floor, Jimmy packed the few clothes he had. As he hurried down the hillside, which was illuminated by the weak light of an incipient dawn, he trembled with feelings of liberation and fear. A few blocks away, he saw another bike leaning against a house. After slinging his suitcase across the handlebars, he pedaled up the hill to the next town. The man to whom he had sold the first bike was happy to give him another twelve dollars for the second. Within an hour, Jimmy, almost euphoric with a feeling of success, was in the rear seat of a Greyhound heading for New York City.

On the trip north, he chattered incessantly to a sailor, telling him fantasies about his rich family in New York. His father worked in television, Jimmy bragged; mostly on "Mission Impossible." He said he had been on a camping trip where he had lost his plane ticket and good clothes. The sailor didn't believe a word of it but listened amiably enough.

As the bus rolled along the New Jersey flatlands, Jimmy got his first glimpse of New York at dusk, when the city's backlit skyline seemed like the silhouette of castles. The roaring, glistening tube of the Lincoln Tunnel was an overture to the noise and vastness of the Port Authority Bus Terminal. As soon as the bus had angled its way into Dock twenty-three, Jimmy disembarked, said good-by to the sailor (who didn't hear him), and fell in with the quickly-moving crowd.

His mind battered by the cacophony, Jimmy hesitated at the top of the escalator that led to the main concourse; in front of him was a swirling, confusing mass of people. His heart began to pound and he couldn't remember what he had planned to do next. After long anxious moments, he remembered the YMCA. That was it; that was where he wanted to stay. He guessed he would live there for a couple of days until he found a job.

Moving toward the center of the concourse, Jimmy found a bewildering number of phone books, each one five times as thick as his hometown directory, their rack occupying three sides of a concrete support column. He started searching through a copy of the Yellow Pages, not knowing the difference between Brooklyn and the Bronx, trying to find the location of the "Y." Whenever another visitor showed impatience at having to wait, Jimmy would back off apologetically.

To a cop, a social worker, or a youth worker, Jimmy would have stood out. But at that moment a trained observer of a different kind was the only person interested in Jimmy; in fact, Jimmy was just what he'd been looking for all day.

The boy's outfit instantly and accurately told the person several things. The well-worn, patched Levis were slung so low over the hips that Jimmy would have been half-naked if he'd sneezed. The crumpled, cheap cotton shirt had two missing buttons, the soiled sneakers might last Jimmy through the warm September, but not much longer. The broken suitcase with its "simulated leatherette-type finish" was held precariously together with a frayed thin rope. The overall picture of the boy and his belongings yelled "Poverty."

Jimmy's frantic searching in the Yellow Pages proclaimed him as unattached. If he'd been looking through the white pages, he might have been looking for the number of a friend, but the Yellow Pages indicated he was looking for a place, not a person.

The observer wasn't much better dressed than Jimmy, but, unlike Jimmy, the man could afford expensive things. Before becoming a pimp, Al—now in his forties—had punctuated his time in the Navy with significant periods in the brig. He had also spent a few years in the Merchant Marine. Moving closer to the boy, he fumbled with some change in his pocket and said, in an offhand way, "You might have trouble finding what you're looking for, son. Some of these sons of bitches rip out the whole page instead of taking the time to write down the number."

Jimmy jumped when he heard the voice but, deciding the man seemed friendly enough, he explained, "I was looking for the number of the YMCA," and added, "I'll be staying there for a couple of days while I look around for a place to live."

Al had heard that story before and thought, "Strike one . . ."

He pondered for a few seconds and then asked, "Which YMCA do you want? Uptown, midtown, or downtown?"

On hearing that there was more than one, Jimmy felt lost again. Appearing disconcerted, his voice quavered, "The closest . . . I guess."

Al said, "That would be Sloane House on Thirty-fourth Street . . . but they're usually crowded even though they've hiked their prices to six bucks a night."

Jimmy was aghast! Six bucks a night!

Al noticed the reaction and thought, "Strike two . . ."

While turning around as if to leave, Al said, "Well, there are cheaper places around than that, of course." Then, as though in an afterthought, he turned back to Jimmy and said, "Hey, I've got an idea! There's a friend of mine who lives just a few blocks from here . . . a boy not much older than you and he knows the city like the palm of his hand. I'll call him if you like and ask if you can stay with him for a couple of nights until you find your way around. I know he won't mind. He's done it before for kids coming in from out of town."

Jimmy stammered, "That would be g-great if you're s-sure he wouldn't mind."

Al smiled reassuringly. "He won't mind! Let's go get a cup of coffee while I call him. And so you won't feel obligated," he added with mock severity, "you can buy the coffee."

He picked up the suitcase, though Jimmy protested, and they started across the concourse to Walgreen's Drug Store. With Jimmy tagging alongside Al, the two looked like father and son. Squeezing in at the counter, Al ordered coffee and doughnuts and then excused himself to go to the phone. While Jimmy sat there, he thrilled to the thought that everything was working out. New York was indeed Fun City! He wondered what Al's friend would be like and whether it would be appropriate to offer him money for staying at his place. At the phone booth, Al dialed a number. When a boyish voice answered, he said, "Strike three . . . and you're in, Steve. I've got us a real winner!"

Steve, at fourteen, was a full-time hustler with three years' experience. Like Jimmy, he had run away from a small town, one of a vast number of youths who crisscross the country every year, living witnesses to every conceivable problem that plagues the nuclear family. Steve, who had also been snared by Al, was now not only hustling for himself and his pimp but also recruiting newcomers. The recruiting included conversion and training.

Jimmy was welcomed to the cheap apartment: a one-bedroom, second-floor walk-up just eight blocks from Times Square. During an hour or so of apparently casual conversation Steve confirmed Al's original evaluation. Jimmy would make the ideal trainee. He met the three basic requirements: he was attractive, unattached, and afraid of the police. Before Al left the apartment, he estimated Jimmy would be ready for the streets within two weeks.

The next day, Steve took Jimmy on a walking tour of midtown Manhattan, showing him places where work could be found. "There are plenty of jobs," Steve asserted, "as busboys, messengers, office boys, or errand boys in the garment district over on Seventh Avenue."

That night Jimmy asked Steve what he did for a living. Steve dissembled, saying he made deliveries for a small electronics company, explaining that he had three weeks off because the place was temporarily shut down for remodeling. They also talked about sex, each one conjuring up amorous adventures with mythical girls.

The following day, filled with excitement and determined to come back to the apartment that night with a new job, Jimmy, alone, looked for a way to make a living. But he met sheer frustration. He was brusquely told he was too young or questioned with suspicion, and always told to go home to his family. It was the first of a series of depressing days.

Steve, however, was always at the apartment evenings to encourage Jimmy, to help him pick out jobs advertised in the newspapers, and to persuade him to go to the far-flung corners of Long Island and the Bronx for interviews. He reassured Jimmy that the same thing happened to everyone. But by now Jimmy was out of funds and Steve was supporting him. He knew Jimmy wouldn't get a job, yet each evening he inflated his expectations with well-timed comments as Jimmy talked about the day's failures, tomorrow's hopes ... and sex.

One particular night, Steve decided it was time to begin Jimmy's initiation. During a stimulating talk, Steve unearthed a pile of pornographic magazines from the bottom of a bureau drawer. Jimmy was fascinated. They showed him things he'd vaguely heard of but never seen: men and women engaged in every possible sexual variation; two men and one woman; two women. While keeping a careful eye on Jimmy's reactions, Steve squeezed himself as he voiced a soft sound of pleasure. Jimmy, too, was visibly aroused and, when he stood up, Steve playfully grabbed at the bulge in Jimmy's pants. That was as far as Steve went; just a quick boyish gesture, but he noted that Jimmy didn't back away.

A few minutes later, Jimmy went to the bathroom. One of the magazines was missing from the table. Steve, his ear pressed to the bathroom door, recognized familiar sounds. He grinned. It was time to put Jimmy to work.

Jimmy came home the next day, again without a job and without any money. Steve listened to the litany of woes as he had listened before, but suddenly—as if he'd just thought of it— he said, "You know, you can always pick up a quick ten bucks or so by letting some guy blow you."

Jimmy was appalled. "I'm no queer!" he protested.

"Neither am I," retorted Steve. "You're not queer if the other guy does the blowing," he explained. "There's plenty of guys in New York who are willing to pay good money to do it. All you have to do is to lie back and pretend you're enjoying it."

Jimmy was only partly convinced. Although he was mostly intrigued, he was still a bit scared. He rationalized, "If Steve does it, it can't be that bad." He still had no idea that it was *all* Steve did for a living.

Two days later, Jimmy felt he had no other option: unwilling to return to his home in West Virginia, he had to go along with Steve's suggestion. After all Steve was his only buddy and he was owed more than money. So Jimmy was nudged into action.

"I've got a guy coming up to the apartment this afternoon," Steve mentioned. "He pays fifteen bucks to blow me and he likes to have guys watch him do it. He'll give you ten bucks just for watching. How about it?" In an understanding tone, he added, "You could sure use the money, I know."

That afternoon, Jimmy stared in fascination at the sight of Steve writhing on the bed. Jimmy had ten bucks clutched in his hand, a stiffness in the groin, and a brand-new career.

Jimmy now works out of a grimy amusement arcade with the perversely appropriate name of *Playland*. Jammed with electronic pinball machines, it is conveniently located on the south side of Forty-second Street between Broadway and

Eighth Avenue. Just around the corner, between Forty-second and Forty-third street, there's an entrance to a labyrinth of subway tunnels that leads to the Port Authority Bus Terminal and a myriad of other points scattered throughout the city.

Around Times Square, amid the glare of pulsing neon, people looking for various diversions mingle with pickpockets, drug pushers, murderers, and hustlers. Unwary tourists, coming upon Times Square, feel the tension and recognize the hostile looks. The wise ones grab their children by the hand and scurry away to safer territory.

On Forty-second Street itself movie houses and adult magazine stores offer pornography; windows display shoddy merchandise. Men, women, and children look, search, evaluate. Drag-queens, believing there is safety in numbers, clatter brazenly by in groups of three or four, glaring defiantly at policemen, also in groups, staring suspiciously while their walkie-talkies squawk in static-loaded gibberish. Female prostitutes, in wigs and tight clothes, blatantly pace their territories or lean against doorways.

In contrast, boy prostitutes are not as easily distinguished, even though they outnumber female hookers five to one. As the chickens dart through the crowds, linger in front of theaters, and talk to their potential clients, they appear to be normal children.

Among the chickens there are slightly more Puerto Ricans than blacks; the population of white chickens is significantly smaller than both. Most of the boys come to midtown Manhattan from slums in the Bronx and Brooklyn; a few come from nearby towns in New Jersey. In *Playland*, as they wait for men, they pour never-ending streams of quarters into the flashing, ringing games.

The chickenhawk, or "john," is an adult male of any age. Unaccompanied, he wanders through *Playland*, stopping only near machines being played by young boys. His searching, appraising look allows them to recognize his intentions. Once eye contact has been etsablished, the first stage of a ritual begins. The boy asks for a quarter. A "No" indicates no interest in that particular boy. With a "Yes," the man makes his interest known. While the boy plays the machine, he and the man look each other over. The man offers encouragement—and increasing interest—with additional quarters.

The second stage is usually initiated by the boy. He says he's hungry and would like to eat. If the adult offers to buy a meal, the boy will usually suggest Tad's, a fast-food restaurant next door to *Playland* where the standard dinner costs just over two dollars. Its rest room is often used for a close-up inspection of the boy's body, on which the final decision of the adult is based. The boy isn't that selective. He wants to make as much money as he can in as short a time as possible.

If the adult and boy agree to use each other, they will then check into a hotel. In that midtown section of New York there are many cheap hotels that depend on the prostitutes for much of their business. Their eight-dollar-a-night rooms are havens for people who want them for only an hour or so.

By the time the chicken and chicken hawk start to undress, the man knows just what he's going to get for the fifteen dollars he must pay. The boy has detailed just what he will and won't do, though it's not uncommon for the "won't do" to be done in return for a supplemental payment. A fledgling, inexperienced chicken permits himself to be the passive partner in an act of oral sex. Soon he will provide other services and eventually play the active role in anal intercourse. He'll also learn how to handle a client quickly in one of the many neighborhood movie houses if his client doesn't want to pay for a hotel room.

Sergeant William McCarthy, a plainclothes cop who knows the street and the chicken business, said: "It's an economic thing with these kids. They'll go to one of the movie houses with the adult and let him play the female role. As far as they're concerned, they're making money and retaining their male pride. Clinically, a case could be made that they're latent homosexuals . . . but they don't think of themselves in that way. Most see it as an easy way to make money."

McCarthy, just turned thirty, has been on the police force for nine years. He is the modern-day conception of the super-cop, the new breed more concerned with social issues than with bashing in heads. When he isn't pounding the streets, he's attending college, working on his Master's degree in social relations.

McCarthy's boss, Captain Lawrence Hepburn, an eighteen-year veteran, heads up the New York Police Department's (NYPD) Central Obscenity Unit, an incongruous name for the section of the Public Morals Division concerned with boy prostitution. Forty-two-year-old Hepburn did his Master's thesis on pedophilia, the sexual attraction of adults to young children.

The two policemen sat in front of City Hall during their lunch hour, oblivious to a chanting mob demonstrating about something or other, and recalled cases they had worked in the past year.

*Hepburn:* "One of the most bizarre was the bishop in the Bronx. Dressed in his official robes, he would hold this special Communion service for young boys. It was all very solemn. The high point of the Communion was when the bishop would lie on a crucifix on the floor . . . arms outstretched . . . and the boys would file past and fellate him."

*McCarthy:* "Wasn't that in Brooklyn?"

*Hepburn:* "No. The Brooklyn bishop was the one that ordained the boys he liked."

*McCarthy:* "We'd better point out that these bishops weren't connected with a 'legitimate' church. They were ordained by one of those mail-order organizations."

*Hepburn:* "We also had a case in Spanish Harlem that was a little unusual. A Puerto Rican adult considered himself something of an expert on voodoo ... and so did a lot of other people. They really believed this guy had the evil eye. He would watch for young kids coming to New York, particularly those that came from small villages in Puerto Rico. If he liked their looks, he'd put a curse on them and the only way the curse could be lifted was to go to bed with him."

*McCarthy:* "Remember the Sea Cadet troop in Jersey? The whole troop had scored with the troop leader. If a boy wanted to join up, that was part of the initiation. He'd make it with the leader and some of the other boys and then be sworn to secrecy."

The action, however, isn't confined to New York City. New York, like other major cities, feels the effects of this problem more acutely than smaller locales because of its size and its attractiveness to runaways. In White Plains, New York, police received an anonymous letter from a concerned parent, followed up on the information, and arrested four men in what they described as a unique call-boy service in that city.

Westchester County District Attorney Carl Vergari said three of the four men arrested shared the profits in the operation of a boys' house of prostitution located on a quiet, tree-lined street in New Rochelle, New York. Customers paid from twenty to twenty-five dollars for sex activity, choosing from at least twenty-five youngsters in the thirteen- to seventeen-year-old bracket. Vergari said that while some of the youths were recruited from New York City, others were brought across state lines from Massachusetts to the split-level home rented by the operators. A neighbor had noticed the unusual amount of boy and adult traffic at all hours of the day and night and notified the police.

After a period of surveillance, a ten-man raiding party, led by New Rochelle police plus deputy sheriffs and a special service squad from the D.A.'s office, smashed down the door at one o'clock in the morning and surprised four adults and two boys aged thirteen and fourteen. According to the charges filed against them, they were performing "unnatural acts." One man was charged with the promotion of prostitution in the first degree and sodomy. Two others were also charged with promoting prostitution, while the fourth was tagged with endangering the welfare of a child as well as with sexual abuse.

The two boys involved were both runaways from Baltimore who had been brought to the house from Boston by one of the operators. His function was to recruit youngsters for the brothel, and he managed, on his recruiting trips, to kill several birds with one stone. He'd travel to Boston twice a month to pick up suitable youngsters at bus-stop hangouts. He'd then head to New York, dropping off the new recruits at the New Rochelle house on the way. Once in New York City, he'd repeat the process, recruiting new boys and delivering them to New Rochelle on his way to Boston. The operator even managed to gain additional funds by illegally picking up relief checks when he was in both New York and Boston.

Vergari wouldn't say how the men shared the proceeds of the business with the youngsters, but he did indicate the boys acted quite willingly and that they were lured to the house on the promise of receiving most of the proceeds. An assistant in the New Rochelle rackets bureau said a quantity of pornographic material showing detailed sexual acts was also seized in the raid.

There is an important point to make regarding these raids and arrests: they usually go unreported by the press. Both wire services, the Associated Press and United Press International, file the stories to their clients (newspapers, radio stations, and television stations), but the stories are always preceded with the cautionary "EDITORS: (NOTE NATURE OF THE STORY)." Editors do . . . and often elect not to use them.

Just as important are the number of cases that don't even reach the arrest stage. The police themselves elect to run the culprits out of town permanently rather than prosecute them— especially when an important adult is involved.

# 2

# Scott
# and the West Coast

*"Are you old enough
to smoke a little grass?"*

There are tightly run organizations in the United States and overseas geared to provide wealthy clients with both pornography and boys. Their operators, like street pimps, recruit and train runaways. But these highly paid entrepreneurs have much higher standards than the street pimps, and use different procedures; their boys will entertain movie stars, prominent athletes, politicians, and, in some cases, heads of state. Jimmy would never qualify for this elite arena, but Scott did.

He stood on the shoulder of Highway 15 just outside a flyspeck town called Beacon Station. His eyes followed the pickup truck that had brought him from Las Vegas as it turned down a farm road toward Crucero. He had wanted to get a ride straight through to Los Angeles, but the traffic rolls quickly along Highway 15 and drivers are reluctant to stop for hitchhikers. So, after waiting for more than an hour in the blistering desert sun, Scott had been grateful when a farmer skidded to a halt in a cloud of swirling dust. Scott was the kind of boy that people feel safe about picking up. Well-dressed and still clean after five days on the road, he presented a good appearance standing there silhouetted in the fading light of evening, his thumb sticking out almost apologetically.

Three grim years earlier, his father had deserted the family. Scott's already harassed mother had tried, but the task of providing for six kids was too much for her. When Scott's fourteenth birthday went unnoticed, he decided to leave. He wasn't a runaway; rather a walkaway. He told his mother he wanted to go to Los Angeles to look for work. There were a few minor protests, but she finally gave her consent, consoling herself with the thought that some kind of government agency would take care of him if he got into any kind of trouble. She even fantasized he might get a job playing his guitar. Scott looked like David Cassidy; maybe he would find work in the movies.

The man in the new Lincoln Continental who picked Scott up after the farmer left him in Beacon Station told him the same thing. He talked knowingly about movies and television. Even though Scott was sure he'd seen the man on TV, he hesitated to ask who he was. He didn't want to sound like a hick from Indiana going to Hollywood to gawk at movie stars. The Lincoln rolled along, swallowing up the single white line that divided the dazzling pavement, swept disdainfully through San Bernardino, and then joined the battle for an island of space as it merged with the freeway traffic in downtown Los Angeles.

By this time, the man knew just about everything there was to know about Scott; enough to realize the boy could be useful. Scott unwittingly had passed his first test. He responded eagerly to the suggestion that they go to dinner after first stopping at the man's house for a shower and a change of clothes.

The house, perched on a private knoll off Mulholland Drive, offered an airliner's view of Los Angeles, glittering below like a pearl-studded oyster bed. It was the most splendid home Scott had ever seen. For the first time, he walked on thick carpets, luxuriated in a sauna, and bathed in a sunken bathtub flanked by a jacuzzi. His hair was still warmly damp as he examined the closet in the adjoining bedroom, a closet crowded with rows of double-knit slacks and expensively-soft denims. Most of the clothes were of Scott's size, and he wondered whether the man had a son his age, perhaps away at school.

As he made his selection, the man walked into the room and handed Scott a drink. "It's a screwdriver," he explained. "Orange juice, with a little vodka to wash away the road dust."

Scott downed two more drinks while he admired the stereo equipment. As the man pointed out the controls on the Marantz 4400, he casually massaged the back of Scott's neck with one hand. Scott didn't flinch or pull away. Why should he? It was a perfectly innocent gesture; a friendly touch that felt good. When the man said it was time to eat, Scott was reluctant to leave—until he saw the Ferrari!

The short ride down the narrow winding roads to Sunset Strip was a completely separate experience. The Dino's exhausts crackled and snarled as the man expertly down-shifted on the tight curves and bellowed with a voice of authority on the short straightaways. On their way to Malibu, Scott was enthralled by the glamorous atmosphere of the Strip. He wanted to be a rich Beautiful Person. He yearned to wear sunglasses at midnight while waiting in front of discotheques.

After a costly and satisfying supper, they drove home by a different route and made a brief stop at a deserted section of beach just past Santa Monica. The man had carefully controlled the amount of liquor Scott drank. He had taken in enough to be mellow, relaxed, compliant, and talkative; not enough to be uncontrollable or obviously drunk.

"Well," the man said laughingly, "you're old enough to drink. Are you old enough to smoke a little grass?" It was a carefully loaded question. A fourteen-year-old boy from Indiana, primed with several drinks, impressed with everything he'd seen and done, eagerly awaiting new experiences and adventures, wasn't going to answer "No."

Scott said scornfully," Are you kidding...?" Besides, he had smoked grass before. Not much, to be sure, but some.

The man sat down on the sand after carefully scrutinizing the beach. He fumbled in his pocket and took out two fat joints. "Here," he said, handing one to Scott. "We can toke up here. There's no one around."

Scott delayed lighting the joint. He wasn't sure he had done it correctly when he'd tried it before, so he surreptitiously watched the man sucking down deep draughts of air with the smoke.

It didn't work too well when Scott first tried it. He coughed and choked and gasped out an excuse about it "going down the wrong way."

The man laughed understandingly. "Take it easy at first," he advised. "This grass is from Colombia and it's very strong."

It was, and by the time they walked back across the sand to the car, it had hit Scott. The walk seemed to take an hour. The outlines of the hills appeared razor-sharp and there were vibrant colors everywhere that he hadn't noticed before. The Dino took on new dimensions. It was fifty feet long, almost alive, as it leaped eagerly through Topanga Canyon toward the San Fernando Valley. Scott laughed with sheer delight when they finally turned eastbound on Ventura Freeway. The engine muted to a throaty rumble as the car sped effortlessly back toward the man's house.

Later, as Scott snuggled between the blanket and the undulating warmth of the water bed, the man slipped in silently beside him. There was no conversation, no questioning, no direction, and no protest. Scott passed his final exam and paid the bill for the evening's entertainment. . . .

Within two months Scott had responded to the carefully orchestrated indoctrination. During the day, he was a student at a fashionable junior high school. In the evenings, he obediently kept appointments made for him by his pimp or, perhaps, posed—sometimes with other chickens—for photographers.

Scott did not get rich, but his pimp certainly got richer. Scott's acquisition brought his mentor's stable of boys to six, four of whom lived with parents, one who stayed with a friend, and the hard-working Scott who still lived at the man's house. Scott wasn't complaining though. He had plenty of clothes and lots of spending money from the twenty dollars he received every time he serviced a client, plus occasional bonuses. Weekends ranged from trips to the mountains to trips to Catalina Island aboard private yachts. Scott was right at home in the most fashionable country clubs and got used to being introduced by his clients as a "nephew" or the "son of a business acquaintance." He played these multi-roles well and grateful clients responded by giving him extra cash or gifts. He politely turned down offers of a more permanent relationship, although some of his friends had accepted similar propositions and had done very well for themselves. Scott reserved that option for a later date. It didn't occur to him that in his highly specialized field his youth was not only his prime asset—it was his only asset.

Scott's period of usefulness and profitability would be short-lived. Although he was growing older, he was, in his world, something of a modeling star. But the chicken pornography market demands a constant supply of fresh talent: new faces, new bodies, and imaginative sex acts. Recruiting was constant, and one source for new recruits would eventually be Scott himself. After all, he was a regular student in junior high school, surrounded every day by possible candidates. He was, by this time, very street-wise about his business and could tell quickly and accurately what boys might be persuaded to enter his profession. He was also coached to look for telltale signs: watch out for a boy who's having trouble at school and at home; if a boy likes school, forget him; if a boy tells you what a great family he has, forget him; forget also the uglies, the fats, the ungainly, the real toughs, the bullies—chances are they won't respond; forget it if they don't smoke a little grass; forget it if they're super-studs with the women; forget it if they're rich.

Boys often experiment with each other sexually, more often than not in the guise of a masturbation contest. Most of this sex play happens once or twice and is then forgotten. A lot of it, however, is repeated and not forgotten. In Scott's case, and in the case of hundreds of other Scotts, it was to be played, hopefully, for a permanent repeat ... and possible profit. Scott knew how to guide, direct, and tempt because he himself had been guided, directed, and tempted.

He would always select a boy about a year younger than himself because boys in school tend to admire the older boys and denigrate the younger. For a younger boy to receive the attentions of an older boy was a heady experience. The younger would brag to his contemporaries about his "buddy." And Scott was someone to brag about. He was a glamorous figure, always dressed in the latest fashions. He lived in a home that was like "Wow! Something else, man!" His record collection was the envy of everyone. Stereo rigs like his had been admired before only in stereo-equipment stores. He always had money and was generous with it. And he always had super grass. Scott lived with his uncle who was really great. And he had no mother to hassle him about being home on time, wanting to know where he'd been and with whom. Scott, in the eyes of other kids, had it made. There were, consequently, plenty of boys who wanted to be Scott's friend, to have what Scott had, and to live as Scott lived. And Scott knew just how they could get it all!

It was a precarious game. If Scott picked the wrong boy and used the wrong approach, that same boy could blurt out what had happened all over school. Scott would then be tagged as a "queer" and would be subject to ridicule. There were several boys in his school so labeled; Scott avoided them like the plague. Sexually, Scott's future could go several ways. He could marry, have children, and an occasional flirtation with a male companion. He could, essentially, settle down into a normal life . . . and many boys like him do. If he should grow up to be reasonably famous, however, he would face a constant problem with all those pornographic pictures floating around. They could haunt him for the rest of his life and could subject him to the constant threat of blackmail. His drive for success could easily be tempered by the existence of the porno art.

On the other hand, Scott could elect to continue his profession, graduating into the ranks of older prostitutes, serving men who like older boys. He might even find a permanent relationship this way. In Scott's world these are the good things that could happen. But there are bad possibilities that can more than offset the good.

On the negative side, he faces the constant threat of being caught and jailed; he faces the constant threat of drugs turning on him instead of turning him on; he faces the constant threat of venereal disease . . . an absolute disaster in his profession. But the real danger he faces is to his mental health: he is living a false life, much like his female counterpart. He is bedding down with some singularly unattractive people and has to cater to their whims and needs, regardless of what these might be.

Scott has to decide what his sexual orientation is. Is he homosexual? He would deny it, saying that while he services homosexuals, he, himself, is not one. Is he heterosexual? He does spend some of his time, and some of his earned money, with girls. This would tend to convince him that he is not a homosexual but a heterosexual using homosexuals to generate his income. But Scott, like most of his peers, is not overly concerned with what he is. He is more concerned with what he can get from his adult companions. They, on the other hand, know what they want.

# 3

# The Chickenhawk

*"Eighteen boys . . . showed up
for the funeral."*

It is, somehow, part of American nature
to paint with a large brush. There is a tendency in our society to
leap endlessly toward simple accusations and simple answers.
This certainly holds true in the societal terms used to describe
the people in this book. Apart from the boy prostitutes, the most
important character in our discussion is the adult.

If you use the generic term, he is known as a child molester,
a label that is hopelessly inaccurate when applied here. A child
molester evokes visions of America's most popular bogeyman.
He lurks in the shadows of public schools and city parks, wearing a dirty raincoat and armed with a pocketful of jelly beans.
He sidles up to unsuspecting, innocent children and carries
them off to his car where he subjects them to a wide variety of
sexual indignities. He's the one we warn our children about, the
stranger to whom they should never talk. He does, of course,
exist . . . but he's not the subject of this book. That individual
is a pedophile, a man with a strong sexual interest in children—
and he often doesn't care much whether the child is a boy or a
girl. It just has to be a child.

Our subject is different. He is described in the dictionary

as a pederast, one who engages in sexual relations with minors. On the street he is called a chickenhawk. The big difference between the pederast and the pedophile is that the pederast described in this book carefully selects consenting boys. He is not interested in force, violence, conversion, or rape. He makes his choice and pays his money.

The chickenhawk defies description. He is short and tall, young and old. He's happily married with a large family. He's the distant cousin; the visiting uncle. He is rich and he is poor. He's the truck driver who delivers the TV set; the professional athlete; the nice guy in the upstairs apartment. He's a doctor, a musician, or a man who comes to read the gas meter. His occupation won't provide the slightest clue to his identity. He cannot be identified by his mannerisms or his voice, so any attempt to warn children about the appearance of a chicken hawk is pointless.

The man quoted on the following pages is from San Francisco. He is happily married, has three teen-aged children, two boys and a girl. Judging by his life-style and his apartment, he probably earns around forty thousand dollars a year. He has a pleasant appearance and, even though he's in his forties, keeps in good physical shape. He is far removed from the man in the dirty raincoat (the one with the jelly beans in his pocket). His business takes him out of town a great deal and he travels to many parts of the United States—to big towns and small. Here's what he had to say when interviewed:

"The trouble is, there aren't enough of us. By that I mean there aren't enough of us who really care for the boys. *Really* care for them. You find that strange? Look, there's no way I could possibly keep count of the number of young boys I've had since the days when I was young myself. I started fooling around with my buddies when I was about ten and I haven't quit. I enjoy it; I love it, but I've never scored with a boy who didn't want to play . . . and that's a helluva lot of boys. I know what you're thinking and I know all the nicknames. It's even put down by some of the gays—but I don't buy any of it. I'm not effeminate, I don't drool, and I don't hang around schools. The only people who know about me are the boys with whom I've scored and a group of friends around the country who are into the same thing.

"You were talking about violence, blackmail, extortion, and things like that. I've never had it happen to me, although I've heard about it happening to others. I pick my kids carefully and I treat them right. Anyone that has trouble probably deserved it. Most of the kids I pay because I want to. I enjoy giving them money. They've earned it and they deserve it and, in many cases, they desperately need it.

"I don't know anything about the organized prostitutes except that they exist. Professional call boys at a hundred bucks a throw aren't my bag. I go for the street kids—the urchins—and the poorer they are, the better. Besides, what does a hundred-dollar number do for his money that I can't get for ten or twenty? I can't see any fun in going to a phone and ordering up a boy I've never seen and then going to a designated place to see what I've bought. Do you know that kind of operation uses wine as a code? For instance, if you order an eleven-year-old light-bodied wine, you are ordering an eleven-year-old light-bodied blond boy?

"I know what I want and I know where to get it and I enjoy playing the game. I guess I like the chase as much as the conquest. The street kids have no inhibitions, no hang-ups, and there are only the two of us involved. Me and him. I rarely take more than one at a time. That's dangerous and dumb and it only works with the very young or if you're in Spain, Mexico, Morocco, or someplace where that kind of thing is popular.

"If I go to a city or town and don't know where the action is, I start at the bus depot, a cheap movie house, or a park. A good indicator is the graffiti on the walls. There's a lot of information there to the experienced reader. Often I'll get directions from another cruising gay. There are also amusement arcades, beaches of coastal towns, YMCA's, public rest rooms, city bus stops or rest rooms in department stores. The best method, though, is cruising in your car.

"You drive around the suburbs in the big cities when the kids are heading downtown; later in the evening they're heading for home. As with the graffiti, there are certain signs to look for. You can tell the wise kid by the way he stands there . . . with a sort of arrogant stance. If he really wants to score, he'll be standing with half a hard-on. It's instantly noticeable if that's what you're looking for . . . but not to anyone else. It's really quite funny if he's a prime piece of property. All the other cars with drivers looking for the same thing start jockeying for position like a Grand Prix start. Cars zap down alleyways and across parking lots to get in position! If they ever legalize boy-cruising, they'll have to have an odd-even-day plan like they use for gas rationing. When you see something you like, you then have to find out if he likes you. These kids have sharp eyes and fairly high standards. I've asked kids if they want a ride and have been turned down after a very careful evaluation. They check you, the way you speak and act, the car and everything else. Then they'll say they are waiting for a friend. Ten minutes later, you'll see them talking to another driver. It's a little irritating then to watch a kid drive off with the other guy.

"Anyway, let's say you picked up your target, he's in the car, and you're going to try to score. Always ask him how far he's going before he asks you. If he asks you first, you're committing yourself to a long haul that might not work out. He might even be a genuine hitchhiker just looking for a ride. Or he might be wise but is going on a date and is just using his experience to get a ride. Tell him you're going a couple of dozen blocks or so. This leaves you the option of saying, 'This is where I turn off. . . .'

"He'll very rarely come right out and say he's hustling. You have to play out the game. He'll say he's looking for a job, or he planned to go to a show but he's broke, or he's wondering how to get some money to buy his mother a birthday gift. If you're an expert, you'll get a lot out of that conversation. Like a price. He has just laid down some financial parameters. Prices early in the evening are going to be higher than later, by the way. Early on, he still has time to look elsewhere.

"With boys over sixteen, it's a little different. Their conversation is car-oriented. They always have a ticket they have to pay or they'll lose their license. Their car needs repair. They're going to be thrown out of their apartment because they can't make the rent. Obviously, you aren't about to pay for rebuilding a clutch or a brake job or a month's rent, but the idea is to contribute to it. The average asking price is twenty dollars, coming down to ten. I've never paid more than twenty, but I have paid as little as seventy-five cents.

"While the boy is talking, he'll be casually squeezing his groin. If you repeat the gesture, you then know you're both after the same thing. The only items left to negotiate are who does what to whom, where, and at what price.

"In most cases, the deal is that he's going to let you blow him . . . and that's that. But it can change after you're in bed and he's all fired up. He might offer to do more for extra money. And at that point, if he's any good at all, you're agreeable. It amuses me that in this enlightened day and age the blow*er* is considered queer and the blow*ee* is considered straight. That kind of rationale is really incredibly stupid because it just isn't that way at all. If a boy lies there and lets a man play around with him and gets hard and has an orgasm . . . the boy has got to like it!

"Another popular misconception is that the boy will run away and tell his friends—or his parents—what you did. I'm sure this has happened, but it's very rare. In the first place, he doesn't want his friends to know what he's into; in the second place, he wants to come back for a repeat performance. It all depends on the way you treat the boys. If you just take them, use them, pay them, and send them on their way . . . that's nothing. But if you invite them back, or take them to eat, or take them to a show, or help fix their bike or whatever; if you show them that you also like them for themselves, then you've both got a good thing going.

"When I'm at home, I play it pretty straight because of the family. But it so happens I've scored with several of my son's buddies since they were in junior high school. I'm not rationalizing what I do—although I guess I really am—but I've never known a boy who's been ruined by sleeping with a man. I have known thousands of cases where boys have been helped by it, particularly those from homes without any semblance of love or affection. If you nurture a boy, help him, and show genuine concern for him, then he'll respond . . . and I don't mean just sexually. I know several boys now around seventeen or eighteen years old who I used to score with when they were much younger. We don't make out anymore, but we're the best of friends and they come to me for advice and help quite often. No money; just talk.

"There was a country judge I knew who was very fond of boys. He was a bachelor and always kept a couple of waifs and strays around the house. He'd feed them, clothe them, send them to school, and help them get jobs. He really helped them. When they were ready to take on the world, he'd send them on their way and take in another. Well, the judge died about a year ago and eighteen boys from all over the country showed up for the funeral. Some were married and brought their kids. Others had hitchhiked to get there. Most of them didn't know each other, but they all knew what the relationships had been and there was much handshaking and introductions all around. Eight of the boys acted as pallbearers, and if anyone had said a disparaging word about the judge, he would have had eighteen angry boys to contend with.

"I don't know what's happening around the country, but there's some kind of change going on. Kids are becoming more and more available. I think it's the 'if it feels good, do it' attitude.

"Last week I left the apartment to go to the store. My wife was visiting her mother and the kids were in school. When I came back to the building, there was the most beautiful boy—about twelve years old—hanging around the lobby. He was neatly dressed and carried a pair of swimming trunks. I asked him if he was looking for someone and he said he was waiting for his parents who live on the ninth floor. He wanted to get into the apartment to change so he could go swimming. I suggested he could change in my apartment and he eagerly accepted. Right at that moment, from the bold, piercing stare he had, I knew I was going to score. He was delightfully immodest when he changed and did a little dance—completely naked—to the music from the stereo while he struggled into his trunks. He thanked me—with that look again—and left. I had a feeling he'd be back on some pretext or another.

"He was back in five minutes, dripping wet, asking to borrow a towel. He readily accepted when I offered to dry his back. He said his legs were sore from the swim and asked if I would rub them. While I was rubbing his legs—he was lying face down with his head in a pillow—his muffled voice said he'd like to make a few bucks to go to a dance that night. Did I have any chores he could do? I said I didn't have any and asked him how much he needed. He said, 'Just three bucks.'

"By this time, I was rubbing his hips and his butt. He reared up and my hand slipped underneath him and grabbed his penis, which was rock-hard. He rolled over and said directly, 'You can have that for three bucks!' I could—and did—and when I was through he said casually, 'Do you ever do that with your sons?' I was shocked beyond belief! 'Of course not!' He nonchalantly announced, 'I do it with my dad all the time.'

"After he left, I called a friend in the building—he fools around, too—to tell him about my find. He laughed and said, 'That's Victor! He doesn't live in the building. He *works* the building, and nearly everyone I know has had him, including some of the straights.'

"Victor, it turns out, has a good thing going. There are over four hundred units in this complex and he has literally dozens of customers here. He goes to some of them on his way to school and others on the way home. He must be making twenty to thirty dollars a day in this building alone! He also has about three or four friends that tag along with him. Funny thing, he is very discreet. I tried to get him to tell me who else in the building he was scoring with. He wouldn't, and said, 'I don't tell them about you, either.' "

This "protection" by the boy seems to be the rule rather than the exception. Police officers across the country report the same phenomenon. When an arrest is made involving an adult and a child, successful prosecution is very difficult for a multiplicity of reasons. Deputy District Attorney James Grodin, in Los Angeles, said, "The boys don't feel they've done anything wrong! We had a case here in Los Angeles where the adult admitted to having oral sex with a twelve-year-old. I spent two hours with the youngster talking about baseball and a hundred other general things to put him at ease. I then asked him if he had sexual relations with the adult in question. The boy emphatically denied it! He seemed genuinely shocked at the suggestion. When I told him the adult had already confessed to eight separate incidents, the boy shrugged and said, "Oh, that! Sure, he blew me a few times, but we didn't have any sex."

When the parents of a boy are confronted with their son's activities, they rarely feel inclined to file a complaint. They fear the publicity. They would have to face their friends and neighbors and the boy would have to face his peer group at school. Many psychiatrists agree that in such cases far more damage is done to the boy by a court appearance than by the trauma of the incident itself.

The fear of public exposure is very real, particularly to the adult. If he's caught in the act with a young boy, the public gets extremely angry—and very hostile. Playing around with kids repulses most people. Should the adult be sentenced to a prison term, he can look forward to a dismal time in the slammer: convicts regard child molesters as the lowest form of animal life and treat them accordingly.

This fear of exposure is multiplied in direct proportion to the size of the town in which the adult—or the child—lives. A large major city offers anonymity, the advantage of being able to lose one's self in the crowd. But in a small town where everyone knows everyone else . . .

Paul's experience offers a prime example. He is in his early thirties and lives in a small, Midwest town. He was born there and his parents still reside there (he lives separately in his own apartment, quite comfortably, on about seventeen thousand dollars a year—not bad in a town of just over ten-thousand population). Paul is well-liked and well-known. His occupation isn't important except to say that it brings him into daily contact with town officials. A confirmed bachelor, he attends parties and other social functions with acceptable dates, so there's never been the slightest hint or suggestion that he might be gay. He was popular in high school, a noted athlete, and shrugs off his bachelorhood with the traditional bit about not having found the right girl yet. He visits his parents as little as possible to avoid the constant urging to "get married and settle down."

Like hundreds of thousands of homosexuals across the country, he leads his double life successfully. His homosexual activities are carried out in a major city seventy-five miles down the road. He likes his partners young, around fourteen or so, but shies away from long-term relationships. There would be several problems with such an arrangement: first, that seventy-five-mile drive, and second, the dangers inherent in any long-lasting relationship. The unexpected solution to this standard dilemma appeared one morning in juvenile court in his home town.

The boy was thirteen, very attractive in a Norman-Rockwell-newsboy sort of way, very alert, intelligent, and streetwise. Although Paul didn't know it at the time, a psychological report described the boy as a conniving kid who took delight, and a great deal of pride, in his ability to manipulate people . . . especially adults. The report also warned that unless the boy were rigidly controlled, he would eventually develop into a full-blown psychopath.

Paul recalled his feelings about the boy: "When I first saw him, he was the perfect composite of the best in all the boys I've played around with. I was sympathetic because he was in court, all alone, on a bum rap, and the only possible course of action left to the court would be to send him to a juvenile home. Even the court was reluctant to do that. He was obviously a bright kid, the kind of kid any father would be proud to introduce as his son. Even though he was very exciting sexually, I wasn't thinking along those lines at the time. My thoughts were about getting the kid out of that court and keeping him out of a juvenile home.

"The judge, who was a good friend of mine, wanted to hold the boy until they could get more information about his background and his family. . . . I arranged to have lunch with the judge, brought up the subject, and casually suggested the boy could stay with me until some type of disposition was made. Well, the judge was delighted! I was regarded as a responsible person and my intervention would save them the cost of holding the boy in the city jail. We met the boy in the judge's chambers and he was given a stern lecture about what was expected of him and how much he should appreciate what was being done.

"He was a runaway from a nearby state and it took about three weeks for our probation department to get the information it needed. It was a typical case. The father had long since left home, leaving the boy, his older brother, and sister to live with his wife as best they could. In two years, the sister was being taken care of by the Salvation Army, the older brother was in and out of jail, and the younger boy—we'll call him Ronny—was stealing cars for joy rides, acting up in school, and generally following in the footsteps of his brother. When Ronny was picked up in our town, it was his fourth arrest for running away. He wasn't going anywhere in particular. He was just running away, looking for a better life. There was no indication in the first probation report of any type of sexual activity either way.

"I can't tell you how great those first three weeks were. He livened up the house so much. There was noise where it was quiet before. There were dirty socks and scruffy Levis all over the place and a perpetual ring around the bathtub. There was no sex, no discussion about sex, no hints or knowing looks. He was just very visibly there. The only physical contact was some rolling-on-the-floor wrestling.

"The first move toward sex came from him, not from me. I was having such a good time playing father that I really hadn't thought too much about sex. The responsibility seemed, somehow, to override it. But this easy relationship ended one night— about two days before he was due in court for a final decision. I was in bed and he came walking in, wearing just his jockey-shorts, to bum a cigarette. He sat on the bed and we talked about various things—I forget what. He finally wound up in bed with me under the covers, still talking. I didn't think much about it. It seemed perfectly natural for him to be lying there, his head on my arm, occasionally stretching across me to get to the ashtray on the night stand.

"The conversation shifted to his background and he was laying some pretty lurid stories on me about his father, his teachers, and his former friends. It was a warm, intimate type of conversation and I remember I was idly playing with his hair as he spoke. I mentioned it was getting late and we should be getting some sleep. He asked—very earnestly—if he could sleep there . . . with me. It was a logical request and, to me, an idyllic situation. I don't think I have ever felt so important to someone as I did at that moment. I turned the light out and he snuggled closer, my arm still around him, his head on my shoulder. After some preliminary squirming, he settled down and then whispered in a very clear and very urgent voice, "Hey! Do you want to fuck me?"

"I was absolutely stunned. Nine thousand things were racing through my mind. It seemed as if I had to make twenty important decisions that instant, each with about twenty options. If I said 'No,' he would be placed in an excrutiatingly embarrassing position. If I said 'Yes,' I could place myself in a tremendous amount of trouble. He had, over the three-week period, invested a great deal of trust in me. Should I throw this away for the sake of sex and then face possible blackmail or—even worse—public exposure? All these questions rocketed in my brain in the space of a microsecond. I was stammering and hemming and hawing to kill time. He made the decision for me with two squirms of his body and a squeeze of his hand. I said 'Yes' and it proved to be a decision that would cost me two days of indescribable anguish.

"It took three minutes to find out that Ronny was no virgin. He knew every possible extracurricular use for every orifice of his body . . . and for mine. That helped some; helped to offset the incredible feeling of guilt I was experiencing. If he had turned around and said tearfully that it was his first time, I think I would have killed myself through remorse. But it wasn't his first . . . and probably not his fifty-first. Ronny had been there before.

"Breakfast the next day was somewhat strained on my part, not his. He chattered incessantly about general things with no indication that anything unusual had happened, grabbed his school books, crashed out the door, and was off to school.

"I spent a dismal day, with long thoughts of what had happened, what could happen, and what would happen. They were not good thoughts. The time went slowly until three-thirty in the afternoon when he should have been home from school, probably with some thoughts of his own. I hurried to the house, walked in, and my worst fears were confirmed. He'd gone! His clothes were missing, but he'd taken nothing from the house. A note, scrawled in pencil, read: 'I'm going to California. I didn't take anything except the cans of beans. Please don't call the cops on me. Ronny.'

"Another mental upheaval! A feeling of relief that—reading between the lines—he didn't plan on telling anyone what had happened. The house wasn't torn up, so there didn't seem to be anger on his part. He hadn't stolen anything, so there seemed to be some respect for me, and the 'Please don't call the cops' said he certainly wasn't going to the police.

"My thoughts were now on another plane: Even though he'd initiated the sex play, I could have stopped it. Did he want to stop? He must have, or why else would he be on the road? The thing that had to be done right then was to find him and talk about it. If he were going to California, then he'd be heading west on Highway 80, if he hadn't been picked up already. If he were stopped by the state police, wouldn't he be tempted to tell all to get himself off the hook?

"I found him sitting alongside the highway about eighteen miles from town. He jumped up when he saw the car approaching from a distance and looked very discomfited when he recognized it. Getting into a conversation was awkward, but I said we should talk about his trip and, if he really wanted to leave, he could. First, though, there had to be some legal arrangements made, otherwise we'd both be in trouble. He agreed and we drove home in silence.

"We talked long into the night and the subject of sex was never mentioned. I fault myself on that. It had happened. We both knew it had happened and it was—at least to me—of paramount importance. But I didn't bring it up, probably because I was afraid I might hear something I didn't want to. Ronny said he had run away because he was afraid he'd be sent to juvenile hall after the probation department found out about his background.

"I ventured, 'What about us?'

"He mumbled, 'I like it here and I want to stay if I can.'

"That was all I needed to know, though, in retrospect, I should have found out much more. Ronny stayed. The court agreed to let me become a 'temporary' guardian for six months, after which it would re-evaluate the idea.

"It worked well and we had sex together again several times. But as time passed, the sex incidents eased off. There was never any discussion about it. When the mood was right, it happened. That was four years ago. We haven't had sex for two years now. It just died out; replaced, I guess, with more of a father and son relationship. Now that we don't do it, we talk about it. Not about us so much as about what he does now. He's very popular with girls and makes out well. Once in a while, he does make out with a buddy. I know about it and he openly discusses it. Ronny has had a profound effect on my life-style. I still take trips to the big city for my own physical needs but not nearly as often as I used to. I suppose I have enough companionship at home to offset the need of seeking it elsewhere."

❀     ❀     ❀

In the cases of Paul and the San Franciscan both men continue to lead their double lives with some degree of security. But, as Paul said (and the San Franciscan agreed), there is always the constant, gnawing fear of discovery. In the case of the San Franciscan, discovery would not be nearly as nerve-shattering as it would be for Paul. If 'Frisco's family were understanding, the adjustment might just consist of moving to another apartment house (although in view of the fact that he already lived in a giant apartment complex, even a move might not be necessary). Since he is a man of means, the chances of a conviction in court would be slim. He has no prior criminal record and could afford a psychiatrist to testify that he would receive counseling. Under California law, however, he would be required to register as a sex offender, which could lead to future problems. It is extremely unlikely he would change his life-style. Instead, he would probably continue to pursue it with greater caution.

Paul's exposure would have quite different results: it would be a complete disaster. There are rarely deals made in small-town courts. If a case gets into court, everyone knows about it. Therefore, any deals that are going to be made have to be made *before* it gets to court. This course of action is often followed in smaller towns. The culprit is confronted with the evidence and is given the option of stealing away into the night, never to return—or facing prosecution. Juries in such cases are often notoriously harsh. Jurors would run the risk of being talked about themselves if they showed any tendency toward leniency. It's one of the shortcomings of small-town juries. Everyone on the jury knows everyone else and this often results in decisions that are not necessarily based on the facts of the case. If Paul were caught elsewhere, what would the discovery do to Ronny? Would he stand by Paul or would he feel betrayed and run again, convinced there just aren't any adults around who are worth a damn? The arrangement is fraught with pitfalls, among them the possibility of emotional disaster for both parties. Some boys are too immature to handle such a situation; others take it in their stride.

Bart is a good example of the teen-ager with an amazing capacity for coping with disaster. He is nineteen now and makes a good living in the booming oil fields of Louisiana, working alongside his younger brother. Bart has been hired out to older men with money since the age of thirteen. He has made three girls pregnant—one of them only twelve years old. He has had syphilis twice, enough cases of gonorrhea to lose count, hepatitis twice, and a long list of kidney and liver disorders. In his younger days, he bought, sold, and used heroin, LSD, marijuana, amphetamines, and barbiturates. He was thrown out of his home four times and ran away on at least six occasions. He has been arrested four times and jailed twice, experienced a list of medical, sexual, and drug horrors that have permanently laid low many a person. There are not many in this day and age who would have survived the disasters of Bart's life. But he did survive medically, and physically, and mentally, and now considers himself in good shape. He is married, has a new son, and is making enough money. It is very unlikely that he'll revert to his old ways, although he admits to an occasional excursion into that past.

"I've done it all," he ponders, "and it was worth it, but I sure wouldn't want to do it again. I still cringe when I think about the number of times I was on the brink of disaster and was pulled out by some miracle."

Unlike most boys with his experience, Bart did not come from a broken home in the classic sense of the term. His family life rollicked along in a manner that fell somewhere between Ma and Pa Kettle and David Copperfield's Mister Micawber. Lots of kids. Lots of disorganization. Not too much in the way of money, control, or discipline but plenty of love. School was a casual phase with low grades leading inevitably to a ninth-grade dropout. Bart was street-wise and had an engaging manner, good looks, and a genuine trust in people. His first successful attempt at sex came when he was ten.

"I never had any trouble with girls and I was getting as much as I needed, which was plenty," he recalls. "I didn't fool around with boys much except for circle jerks at camp and contests to see who could come first."

His initial homosexual experience came just after his fourteenth birthday. It wasn't with a friend but with his best friend's father, and Bart recounts: "He didn't seduce me. I seduced him and I still don't know why." As he remembers, he was staying overnight at his friend's house. The entire group of boys was tired after a long day of hunting. "My buddy and everyone else had gone to bed. His father was lying down in his bed and I was sitting there on the edge of the bed rapping about guns. I don't remember whether he asked me to do it or whether I volunteered or whether anyone said anything, but I started rubbing his back. When I got down around his waist, I could tell he was getting turned on. That was turning me on. The next thing I knew I was in bed with him and backing in to him."

It was Bart's first time, but it wasn't the first time for his friend's father. Bart says, "When it was all over, he was really embarrassed. He told me he often did it, but never with his son's friends. I guess he was worried I'd tell his son, but that didn't occur to me."

It's possible that Bart's first experience might have led him to another area. About a year later, Bart, in a moment of candor, told an older brother what had happened. He mentioned no names. Bart's brother was very interested because he was running a call-girl service in New Orleans and would, on occasion, get requests for a boy. He suggested to Bart that he might want to consider making himself available. Bart recalls he didn't like the idea much, but the offer of money—a hundred dollars at a time—was too tempting. It didn't work, however. First of all, the hundred dollars was an "asking" price. Bart would sometimes get fifty, more often thirty dollars, and half of that would be kicked back to his brother. Life at home was becoming a problem. His parents were asking questions: Why was he spending so much time in the nearby city with his brother? What was he doing? Where was he working? It became a life of short-haul travel and a growing web of lies.

"I never really liked it," Bart mused. "I would never know who I was going to bed with. I didn't like any of them. When it's with a stranger, it's like being with an animal."

So Bart quickly learned two methods of appeasement: he learned to use drugs (courtesy of his brother) to make his actions easier to take, and he learned new sexual techniques. "I was just like a real prostitute," he exclaims. "I learned the things to say and do so they'd get their rocks off quickly and I could get the hell out of there."

Bart was put out of action by syphilis. "I didn't know you could get it from another guy then! I know better now," he said ruefully. From that point on, Bart was on a downhill medical slide. Syphilis was closely followed by hepatitis, compounded by his first case of gonorrhea.

"I just bailed out of there and went back home," he said. "I didn't know what the hell to do or who to turn to for help. If you go to a public-health vd clinic, they want to know where you contacted vd so they can contact the other person. I was afraid they'd be able to tell I got it from a man and not from a woman."

So Bart went to his buddy's father—back to where it had started—and blurted out the entire story. The father acted promptly. Bart was treated by a private physician and was eventually cured of the social diseases. The drugs, particularly the heroin, were a different problem, one that called for therapy, not medicine. Again, it was his friend's father who came to his aid.

"He had some kind of talent," Bart says. "I could sit and talk to him about anything at all and he'd have the answer. If he didn't have an answer, he'd say so, and then find out where to get it. I think that time I really loved him and I know that I do now."

After a year of advice and guidance, Bart had kicked heroin and pills, and wouldn't look at a drink except "maybe a beer once in a while." He says his friend's father guided him into a life of normalcy, encouraged his marriage, and was always available when he needed help or advice.

"He lives at the other end of the country now," says Bart, "and I haven't seen him in three years. We never write because I don't like to write letters 'cause I don't know how. Once in a while, the phone will ring, and when I answer it, he'll say, 'Hey Bart ... fuck you!' and hang up. It makes me feel real good because I know he still thinks about me."

# 4

# Houston and
# Father McGinnis

*"Sixty dollars is pretty heady stuff
for a thirteen-year-old."*

It is pointless to repeat in any great detail the story of the Houston mass murders that shocked the nation —and the world—in August, 1973. Twenty-seven young boys were assaulted and brutally murdered by a trio of active sadists. There are strong indications that twenty-seven wasn't the total of those killed, but when police had exhumed that number, they decided to leave bad enough alone. Besides, the press had already bestowed the "largest mass murder in United States history" title on the Houston slayings.

It was the Houston story, however, that first screamed to the general public that there were adults using very young boys for sexual adventures. It was the Houston story that triggered a flurry of investigative activity by police departments across the country. And it was the Houston story that confirmed in many minds the often-suspected thought that "all queers fool around with kids"—an idea unsupported by fact. Dean Corll, Wayne Henley, and David Brooks, collectively, set the gay community back about ten years.

And it was from the south-Texas city that two facts directly related to what this book is about, emerged: the first is the fact that police estimate the unholy trio had actually had sexual contact with possibly three hundred young boys, exclusive of the twenty-seven they murdered. The second fact is that, following the murders, street hustling—and the buying and selling of boys—in Houston didn't diminish as one would imagine. Indeed, it increased. Larry, a thirteen-year-old hustler, reported his business doubled overnight.

Larry found out from his school friends that his body had a marketable value. He had the added advantage of looking much older than he actually was and, therefore, was less subject to suspicious glances from police officers late in the evenings. His first foray into Houston's gay world was basic and uneventful. He was picked up by a man and offered money to submit to oral copulation. They went to the man's apartment, Larry lay down on the bed, and fifteen minutes later he was fifteen dollars richer. He remembers he disliked the man who performed the act, but also that he liked the act itself—enough to repeat the performance four more times that night.

By the time he returned home, he had sixty dollars in his pocket, more money than he ever had before at one time. Sixty dollars is pretty heady stuff for a thirteen-year-old from a poor home in Houston . . . or from anywhere for that matter. So Larry went into hustling full time. In any major city, the flesh-market is open twenty-four hours a day. There are the early-morning buyers on their way to work, the lunchtime crowd, and the really big business in the evening.

Larry learned the game well . . . and learned it quickly. By the time he reached his fourteenth birthday, he had a list of steady customers, and had to schedule his "free" time carefully. It's quite possible that as Larry serviced one of his regular clients on one side of Houston, Dean Corll was spread-eagling another boy on his "torture board" on the other side of town. But Larry knew nothing of this. He did know that his sexual offerings were becoming more advanced and esoteric. He was no longer just a "blowee." He had to offer more and so he played the receptor role in anal intercourse if that was demanded—and paid for. Larry also realized he was beginning to enjoy his work and looked forward to new, vicarious thrills.

He backed off when Corll and Henley became the talk of the town, figuring the heat would be on and the customers would scurry underground. But they didn't, and in a matter of days Larry was back in business. Perhaps a little more cautiously, but back in business nevertheless. Now there was a new fear, a new element to contend with—the fear of violence. He says he tried to get out of the business by raising his prices, hoping the demand would drop—which would be very unlikely. If he really wanted to quit, he would have. But the attraction of money, coupled, perhaps, with the vicarious delights that went along with it, was too strong. Larry didn't get out; he just got richer. The pressure was tremendous. He couldn't show this display of wealth at home and thirteen-year-olds rarely think about savings accounts. He couldn't spend his money, so he gave a great deal of it away to friends. Some were told how he earned it, but Larry didn't want to share that secret with too many for fear the street action would become competitive. What he really needed though was security. He looked hard for it and finally found it with Father Jack McGinnis, a short, chubby Catholic priest who had a way with street kids—regardless of how horrendous their problems.

McGinnis is a street priest with a parish in one of Houston's poorest barrios. For twelve years he's been Chaplain of the Harris County Juvenile Probation Department Detention Home and, in that role, has counseled hundreds of troubled youngsters. For three years he operated Project First-Step, a halfway house for runaway pre-teens, until he was forced to shut it down because of a lack of funds. McGinnis knows the street scene inside out and is neither shocked nor dismayed by it. He is concerned about it. He bases his help and advice on practicalities, rather than religious dogma, and settles for a high percentage of success.

When I went to see him, he leaned back in his creaky, battered chair and talked about the young street hustler and his life:

"You have to look at every aspect of it, from what's documented as the 'peer-queer transaction,' where the kids do it for money, and that's all, and never turn out to be gay, to those who are gay and go into it because of money only to find they enjoy the life. These are the two ends of the pole. . . .

"I'm talking about the boy who goes on the street and the man who goes on the street to hustle kids—the chicken and the chickenhawk. I've concluded from my experience that the boy who becomes involved generally does so because he's heard about it from other boys; heard there is a ready source of money there. He wants money. He may not need it, but he wants it and just goes to see what it's all about. Sometimes the boy's lured into it, almost unexpectedly. He's just on the street and he's propositioned. He goes into it rather quickly and then continues.

"I think one hundred percent of the boys I have talked to who have become involved in street hustling either had no father because of death, or because the father and mother were divorced. In a few cases, the boy's alienation from his family existed—even if the father was home—because there was no meaningful relationship with the father. I think that has an awful lot to do with this whole situation. I was asked on NBC's 'Tomorrow' show if this was a causative factor. I don't know; I do know it is a factor . . . an important one.

"What about the chickenhawk? I've known only a few men who were actively involved in street hustling and I haven't been able to get an awful lot of information from them. But gay people I've talked to—people who are actively gay, involved in what I would call the 'open' gay community—frown upon this kind of solicitation. They don't approve of it. The men who are involved in street hustling generally are not members of this open gay community. Many chickenhawks are, as you found out, married and have families. I would really venture to say that the deepest radical motivation—when I say radical I mean the causative motivation—of both the men and the boys is the need for affection, for intimacy. This is the driving force behind most pedophiles. Somewhere in their lives they've been alienated to such an extent that they don't have the meaningful intimacy that they desire with people. So it's easier, it's a little more exciting, perhaps more fulfilling to have this with a child.

"The boy may not go looking for intimacy, but once he experiences it he enjoys it, even if it's a weird type of, you know, sadism or whatever. The boy's sexual experience is not enjoyable just because of the physical feeling—the expression of orgasm—it's also enjoyable because of its intimacy.

"Now the desire for intimacy is not bad; is not in itself evil. If we can see that a person has been alienated from intimacy—not sexually, but merely personally, in relationships with other people—then an awful lot of the destructive direction in which this desire for intimacy goes may be avoided. And that's what we, in our effort to help, concentrate on. So we're working with kids and we're working with adults. We're concerned about their behavior; we're concerned about their lives; we're concerned about their depression or destructiveness, or whatever. I think we need to look at the roots of alienation. Many psychiatrists and psychologists have said, basically, the very same thing in different terms. The words 'roots of alienation' mean something to me, something our juvenile justice system doesn't understand.

"Let me be specific. When I find a boy who's been hustling

on the street I don't say, 'Why are you hustling?' He can't answer that. Instead, I begin to look at his early life. I don't want to say, 'Look, if you keep hustling, it's never gonna get you anywhere.' Most of the kids find out it never ends up being worthwhile because it is very exploitative. I ask, 'What's going on in your life? How are you feeling?' The direction I take is toward finding a place—either with me or with somebody else—toward finding a person to help reconcile the deep hurt this youngster has experienced through alienation; toward supplying the intimate relationship he needs in order to feel valuable and loved and, therefore, make him able to love. If we find that, if we supply that, then his behavior is going to change. And it's going to change without even talking about it."

*Chapter*

# 5

# A Tale of
# Two Cities

*"Two of the five indicted
were Boy Scout leaders."*

### IDAHO UNDERWORLD

*Boise, Idaho (pop. 50,000), the state capital, is usually thought
of as a boisterous, rollicking he-man's town; and the home of
the rugged Westerner. In the downtown saloons of the city
a faint echo of Boise's ripsnorting frontier days can still be
heard, but its quiet residential areas and seventy churches
give the city an appearance of immaculate respectability. Recently, Boiseans were shocked to learn that their city had sheltered a widespread homosexual underworld that involved some
of Boise's most prominent men and had preyed on hundreds
of teen-age boys for the past decade.*

When this story appeared in the December 12, 1955, issue
of *Time* magazine, it no longer upset Boiseans. They had already been shocked a month earlier when the scandal made
front-page headlines in their local newspaper, the *Idaho Daily
Statesman.* They were disturbed that what they regarded as a
local "monster" story was now being trumpeted to the rest of

the world. A similar story, making headlines today, would probably provide brisk conversation for four or five days until replaced by something more sensational; but this was 1955, in Boise, Idaho, and it kept the town talking for fifteen months while it suffered the tortures of the damned. Before the scandal was finally laid to rest, a list of 500 suspects had been compiled, 1,472 people were interviewed, the chief of police was fired, and eleven men were sent to jail with sentences ranging from six months to life imprisonment.

Ten years later John Gerassi, a former *Time* editor, decided to research the story. His book, *The Boys of Boise*, revealed that the true causes of the scandal "involved politics and economics as much as personal idiosyncrasies and personal ambitions."

After news of the "rampant" homosexual activity broke in Boise, panic set in and there was wild rumormongering, general hysteria, and strong evidence of injustice. The father of one of the juvenile witnesses was murdered by his own son; the Vice-President of the Idaho First National Bank was sentenced to a seven-year prison term; families were split apart; individuals left town overnight; feuds were started; and political ambitions were either realized or shot down in flames.

The wave of paranoia that swept through Boise has never quite receded; the word "homosexual" still gets adverse reaction in town. The entire situation might well have been handled in a rational, adult manner if the local newspaper had acted responsibly and taken a mature leadership position, but it didn't. On November 3, a month before the *Time* article, the *Statesman* had published this editorial:

CRUSH THE MONSTER

"Disclosure that the evils of moral perversion prevail in Boise on an extensive scale must come as a distinct and intensely disagreeable shock to most Boiseans. It seems almost incredible that any such cancerous growth could have taken root and developed in our midst.

"It's bad enough when three Boise men, overhauled and accused as criminal deviates, are reported to have confessed to violations involving ten teen-age boys; but when the responsible office of the probate court announces that these arrests mark only the start of an investigation that has only 'scratched the surface,' the situation is one that causes general alarm and calls for immediate and systematic cauterization.

"The situation might be dismissed with an expression of regret and a sigh of relief if only one could be quite sure that none other than these three men and ten boys have been infected by the monstrous evil here. But the responsible court officer says that only the surface has been scratched and that partial evidence has been gathered showing that several other adults and about 100 boys are involved.

> So long as such possibility exists, there
> can be no rest...."

The purpose in recapping Boise's 1955 story is not to reopen wounds but to illustrate what can happen to a sizable conservative community faced with the problem of homosexual activity and guided by an irresponsible press. Wayne Kidwell, a Boisean who was a high-school student when the scandal broke, recalls, "We talked about nothing else and it became kind of a game guessing who was involved and who wasn't." Kidwell, now the state Attorney General, said, "If the same thing happened today, the reaction in Boise would be quite different. The people here would take it in their stride and would be able to cope with it, since they've heard so much about it happening in other cities." He added, "The 1955 scandal is still talked about, but the conversation is usually accompanied with some laughter."

Boise, Idaho, was lucky. The city had its scandal and that was the end of it.

Waukesha, Wisconsin, was not so lucky. A scandal similar to Boise's hit the town in 1960 and was repeated in 1974.

On September 7, 1960, Waukesha police announced they had arrested ten persons on various sexual perversion charges following a crackdown on disorderly conduct in the town's Frame and Cutler parks. Included in the roundup was the Dean of Men at Carroll College, a Roman Catholic priest from nearby Milwaukee, and a local dentist. The college administrator was married and had one child; the dentist was also married and had two teen-age children. District Attorney George Lawler said the activity at the parks fitted into a developing undesirable pattern throughout the county. He added, "This thing can be potentially dangerous."

As the investigation continued, so did the arrests. Five days later, an osteopathic surgeon and his roommate were arrested on charges involving a young boy. A week after that, a Waukesha physician was also arrested and charged with taking indecent liberties with a fifteen-year-old boy. This was followed by the arrest of yet another physician on a similar charge with a different fifteen-year-old.

Unlike Boise, Waukesha stayed intact and, considering the extent of the scandal, all the men charged were handed relatively light sentences of up to two years' probation. The first physician arrested was restored to his hospital position after a Marquette University psychiatric evaluation report found no problem that would interfere with his practice of medicine.

It was at least ironic that the hospital in question was the Waukesha Memorial Hospital because, fourteen years later, a similar scandal involving the administrator of the same hospital rocked Waukesha. It was also significant that this time, Waukesha's scandal was destined for big headlines from an over-zealous press, just like Boise's.

The residents of Waukesha were dumbfounded when they heard that Robert M. Jones, president of Waukesha Memorial Hospital had committed suicide on July 7, 1974. The forty-eight-year-old bachelor had been a highly respected and honored member of the community for more than fifteen years. A neighborhood youth found Jones sitting in his car in the garage, the doors sealed with towels. Waukesha County Coroner Donald J. Eggums said the ignition of the car was turned on, but the engine had quit running. Eggums ruled the death as a suicide. No note was found and—at that time—the reason for the suicide puzzled everyone. Or nearly everyone....

Two months later, five local men were arraigned on more than sixty counts alleging improper sexual behavior with minors. District Attorney Richard B. McConnell characterized Robert M. Jones as "the apparent focal point of a homosexual ring which had enticed and contaminated many small boys as young as eight years old ranging up to sixteen." Two of the five indicted were Boy Scout leaders; one, the leader of a troop that spent a three-day camp-out on Jones's land about two months before his death. Some of the improper activities were alleged to have taken place at the scout camp.

On July 11, the coroner ordered an inquest into Jones's suicide. Donald Eggums said he had no doubts the death was a suicide by carbon-monoxide auto exhaust, but he wanted information regarding a party held at the Jones's home the night before his death. Eggums had heard that Jones had threatened to kill himself at the party after becoming angry at a ten-year-old boy who wanted to leave with one of the thirty-five guests.

The coroner's inquest triggered a local political hassle. District Attorney McConnell refused to provide Eggums with an attorney. The coroner had requested counsel since, he said, a routine investigation would not be sufficient because of the need for sworn testimony. As Eggums put it, "This is too big for an ordinary investigation." He said the inquest would center on the possibility of extortion and a possible "community problem" raised by the reported presence of three boys aged ten to fifteen at Jones's party. By this time, the Waukesha County Sheriff's Department was conducting its own investigation, and on August 5, a John Doe inquiry into the events leading up to the suicide was begun before Circuit Judge William E. Gramling.

When the inquiry was first announced, McConnell was careful to say the probe was "not intended to dig into the private life of a deceased person." But it did, and less than a week later, McConnell told the Milwaukee press that Jones "had led a double life as a homosexual and was involved in the contamination of many small boys." The secret inquiries took place in a seldom-used courtroom on the third floor of the courthouse with sheriff's deputies guarding the corridors. McConnell said that Judge Gramling had issued an order that witnesses were not to be contacted or interviewed by the press, and that they were to be protected from photographers, tape recorders, and "other journalistic devices." The purpose of the probe, said McConnell, was to determine whether laws relating to sexual perversion, indecent liberties with a child, and contributing to the delinquency of a minor had been violated and, if so, by whom.

From that point, the town was plunged into political turmoil much the same way as Boise, Idaho, had been. Charges were followed by counter-charges and the pros and cons of each were debated in the newspapers. The press said prominent persons in the case were being protected (much like Boise's), a charge hotly denied by the District Attorney. There were leaks to the press by "unnamed sources" and by August 14, the pieces started to fall into place.

Five men, all acquaintances of Jones, were charged in

county court with a total of sixty-one criminal complaints. Mc-
Connell said he was satisfied that the investigation (in which
twenty-six people—mostly juveniles—testified before Judge
Gramling) had covered all the criminal activities. McConnell
also said the homosexual activity involving juveniles had cen-
tered at Jones's home and apparently had been going on for
some time. McConnell noted with concern that there had been
no complaints by either the juveniles or their parents.

Referring to the Boy Scout camp-out, the district attorney
said a number of the charges were based on incidents that
occurred there when two of the five men charged were running
the camp. Many of the boys were given beer and liquor from
which some became intoxicated, some became ill. The probe
exposed the fact that there had been sixteen separate "indecent"
incidents involving fourteen boys. In one reported incident at
Jones's home, the boys were swimming nude when they were
joined by a thirteen-year-old girl who also removed her bathing
suit at Jones's request. According to information given at the
inquiry, Jones then tried to encourage sexual misconduct, but
nothing came of it.

Then a "reliable source" told the *Milwaukee Sentinel* that
the five men charged with the offenses were just "the tip of the
iceberg" and added, "The generals are free and the second lieu-
tenants are being prosecuted." The same source also shed some
light on just what had happened at the party at Jones's home.
Jones had threatened to kill himself if a ten-year-old boy left
the party with two other men. Since there were from thirty to
thirty-five men at the all-male party, the source said, it was
highly unlikely that those attending were unaware that illegal
activities were going on "when they accepted drinks from a ten-
year-old boy." The source also said the homosexual ring may
have been responsible for at least one other suicide. (This referred to the death, a year previously, of a former food-service
administrator at the Waukesha hospital. Forty-four-year-old

Rome Taft had committed suicide by shooting himself in the head at a Milwaukee motel while being sought by Waukesha police on a morals charge involving a fourteen-year-old boy.)

The *Sentinel*'s source added another fillip to the story, saying Jones's homosexual ring may have been formed ten years or more earlier. Referring to the first Waukesha scandal in Frame Park, the paper's informant pointed out that the participants had all worn white shoes as a means of identification, while Jones had used a series of flags, flown from a flagpole at his house, as signals to invite selected friends over.

Like Boise's, the Waukesha scandal finally died. A Boy Scout official, H. W. Peabody, Scout Executive for the Potowatomi Council, announced that the two Scout leaders would no longer be certified and would be removed from their positions. Another of the men charged with sexual perversion had been hired to teach at a school for mentally retarded children. The school superintendent said he would not be allowed to teach until he was cleared of the charges.

And that might take some time. As of October 1975, those indicted had just reached the preliminary hearing stage and a spokesman for the Waukesha District Attorney's office said, "It has all the earmarks of a long-drawn-out trial." District Attorney Richard B. McConnell had already been defeated in his bid for re-election.

PART

# II

# THE
# CAUSE

# 6

# The History
# of Boy Prostitution

*"In Saigon the boys work
as 'basket-boys.'"*

Boy prostitution is not a product of our turbulent times. It is not the result of sexual permissiveness. It is an element of the American way of life that has been there all along and is now surfacing with the growing acceptance of homosexuality.

The history of boy prostitution goes as far back as any researcher cares to trace. There's abundant evidence of its existence in early literature, plays, poems, murals, and other works of art. Generally, its heyday is associated with the Greco-Roman empires, when slavery was so common it provided ideal conditions for homosexual practice. It seems that the Greeks' general approval of homosexuality influenced the Persians and was then transmitted, together with other Greek traditions, into the Roman Empire, where boy prostitution became quite common. It became fashionable for wealthy Roman families to provide their sons with young male slaves to use as sex partners until such time as the sons got married. But while the Romans' use of boys was interlocked with slavery, male brothels, and street hustling, the Greek approach was quite different.

The Grecian concept of the relationship of boy to man was one of pupil to teacher. Indeed, in the Doric dialect the common word for "lover" was actually "inspirer," which indicates that the adult was also responsible for the boy's well-being in every way. What is not generally known is that the Greeks drew a distinct line between sexual activity with children and sexual activity with older youths. References in Greek literature to boy prostitution were always to sexually mature boys; boys who had reached the age of puberty. In ancient Greece, sexual intercourse with sexually immature children was punished severely. To understand the Greeks' love of boys you have to take a look at the Greeks' ideal of beauty. Hans Licht in his *Sexual Life in Ancient Greece* explains it this way: "The most fundamental difference between ancient and modern culture is that the ancient culture is male throughout and that the woman comes only into the scheme of the Greek man as mother of his children and as manager of household matters. Antiquity treated the man, and the man only, as the focus of all intellectual life. This explains why the bringing up and the development of girls was neglected in a way we can hardly understand; but the boys, on the other hand, were supposed to continue their education much later than they do now."

The most peculiar Greek custom, according to our modern ideas, was that every man attracted to him some boy or youth and, in the intimacy of daily life, acted as his counselor, guardian, and friend and prompted him in all manly virtues. This custom prevailed especially in the Doric states, and it was so much a matter of course that it was considered a lack of responsibility if a man failed to acquire a young ward. It was also considered a disgrace to a boy's family—and to the boy—if he were not selected and honored by the friendship of an older man. Once this selection was made, the adult was solely responsible for the actions and the upbringing of his young charge and shared with him both blame and praise. Indeed, Plutarch tells of one boy who was working out in a gymnasium and was hurt. When the boy cried out in pain, his older friend was punished. In Plutarch there is a continued emphasis on the relationship between man and boy; it was the most masculine and desirable one and was directly responsible for the Greeks' physical prowess on the battlefield. Plato opined that an army made up of lovers of this type, fighting at each other's side, could overcome the whole world.

While many Greek writers represented homosexuality as enobling and normal, modern-day experts still disagree as to whether this reflected the view of Greek society in general or just that of the Greacian elite. There is also disagreement as to whether the relationship between boy and man was primarily sexual or philosophic. But while homosexuality thrived, and was fully acceptable by the Greeks, it was seldom the exclusive channel of love for either man or woman.

The first evidence of boy prostitution appears in Roman history, at least as far as the current definition of the word "prostitute" applies. Most Roman cities had houses of boy prostitutes to provide for the needs of the poorer Romans. Brothel operators would send teams of agents to search the slave markets, looking for attractive young boys (often as young as three years of age) for purchase and training. They were then placed in special schools and brought up with the belief that their sole function in life was to provide sexual enjoyment to adult males who had the money and the inclination to pay for their services.

One of the most famous of these youths was a product of such a training school. Emperor Hadrian's Antinous so completely captivated his master that statues of the boy were set up all over the Roman Empire; several of them can still be seen

in museums around the world. While these boys were prostitutes (available for whatever the paying customer had in
mind), they were primarily slaves, since they were operating
by direction and not by choice.

Because the Roman legions were constantly traveling,
prostitution flourished. Politicians would find themselves transferred on short notice and would not be able to take their families and their retinue of servants with them. Military leaders
were similarly on the move across the country. Businessmen
would find themselves in the provinces for months on end. It
was this movement of population, coupled with the readily
available slaves, that provided an ideal market for prostitution.

Street hustling in the major Roman cities was quite common. In Rome itself the center of activity was the Colosseum,
where hordes of young boys stand waiting for customers who
had been stimulated by the circus inside, which, in the latter
days of the Empire, always contained sexual elements. Both
boy and girl prostitutes were ready and waiting to take advantage of interested customers.

Refreshment stands, often featuring obscene dances to
heighten the sexual mood of the crowd fresh from the circus,
would be erected in and around the arcades of the Colosseum.
Boys would display their wares by raising their tunics to show
their genitals. Once a customer had made his choice, he would
be led to a nearby cubicle covered with a curtain to provide at
least a modicum of privacy.

Roman soldiers (who were generally bisexual) were a
special target for the young hustlers. The prevailing Roman attitude was that girls provided only a partial outlet for sex and
that boys were necessary for a well-rounded program. Since
Roman soldiers were permitted to keep young boys captured in
battle, it was not unusual for three or four Roman soldiers to
jointly provide a boy's food and keep in exchange for the use
of his body. Many a young boy, not previously exposed to pros-

titution, had his first forced homosexual experience in a Roman army tent.

The situation over the years hasn't changed much either in terms of activity or locale. Alfred Kinsey toured Europe as an observer in 1955 and found the Colosseum area was just as promiscuous as it had been in its earlier days. Kinsey's associate, Wardell Pomeroy, in his biography of Kinsey, described the scene this way:

"At the time Kinsey was in Rome, the Colosseum was the center for sexual activity. Its dark passageways, innumerable niches and corners made it an ideal place. There was an altar at one end, with a perpetual candle burning in memory of the martyrs, and on the first night Kinsey was there it happened to be a holy night. He witnessed the weird spectacle of people holding services at the altar while unrestrained sex was going on all around them. Kinsey saw more than thirty couples in every kind of sexual encounter, from petting to intercourse.

"Many different kinds of people were cruising the Colosseum—prostitutes, homosexuals, and those looking for a variety of sexual encounters."

Pomeroy added that Kinsey thought the most notable aspect of these activities was the absence of violence, which could be expected in a similar American scene. Kinsey also commented on another area of homosexual and heterosexual activity in Rome: the famous Spanish Steps. He noted that the homosexuals around the Steps seemed older than those at the Colosseum. At the former they ranged between sixteen and twenty, while at the latter there were many as young as thirteen or fourteen.

Kinsey found Naples even more uninhibited than Rome. Pomeroy recounts that Kinsey found it possible to observe any number of people hunting for sex at any hour of the day or night. A prime area was the famous Galleria, where roving bands of small children would approach visitors and offer to

take them to girls; if that didn't work, they would offer boys—
even their younger or older brothers, and finally themselves.
Pomeroy reports that Kinsey saw males from thirteen to fifty
exhibiting themselves in the public toilets in parks and at railroad stations, showing they were ready for sexual contact.

In earlier days Neapolitan activity is mentioned in the
*Satyricon* and carefully detailed in Roger Peyrefitte's *Exile of
Capri*. Peyrefitte says that when the Spanish ruled Naples,
their troops were billeted in Neapolitan homes. Families with
both sons and daughters would encourage the sons to make
sexual advances to the soldiers in the hope of diverting attention
from the daughters, thereby protecting their purity. Over the
years, Naples developed a reputation as a haven for pederasts,
attracting them from all over Europe. During World War II,
devastation and its resultant poverty pushed boy prostitution
to an all-time high in Italy, as it did in Germany.

Naples today is still a must for touring pederasts. Although
organized houses of boy prostitution have either vanished or
gone underground, local beaches, movie houses, and certain
hotels still provide havens for the activity. Single men arriving
at transportation centers are often approached by tour guides
offering a hotel room complete with a boy. Kinsey noted that in
Rome a bellboy who came to the room was satisfied with a tip,
while in Naples they might sit down and make it clear they
would be glad to stay for other purposes.

It should be said that Pomeroy makes it apparent Kinsey
was not insensitive to other aspects of life in the Italian cities.
He states that Kinsey's journal speaks often of the poverty in
Naples and other parts of Italy, and goes on to say: "Kinsey
was well aware that part of the abundant sexuality directed
toward him and any other obvious American was motivated by
the desperate need for money."

The need for money seems to be the common denominator
in nearly all cases of boy prostitution both in the United States

and abroad. But poverty abroad compared to poverty in the U.S. is quite a different matter. Very often in the poorer foreign countries the word "poor" equates with starvation and desperation. In many underprivileged countries it is possible to literally buy a boy on a semi-permanent—or even a permanent—basis.

A news report from Sri Lanka (formerly Ceylon) says children of plantation workers on the island are being sold into slavery for less than five dollars apiece. A reporter there for the *London Sunday Times* could have purchased an eight-year-old boy in May, 1975 for forty rupees or about $3.85. The reporter said the boy, Raju, was one of hundreds of children being sold by their hungry parents, who work on the tea and rubber plantations for about seventeen dollars per family per month. When the reporter asked the mother why she was selling her son, she said, "Dry season. Very little work. No food many days. Now we buy some." The reporter said he gave the woman one hundred rupees and told her to keep her son.

This type of story from impoverished countries is nothing new, particularly on the Indian continent. The railroad stations in Karachi, Bombay, and Calcutta are teeming with boys of all ages ready and eager to offer a wide variety of sexual services for mere pennies. India has, for hundreds of years, had a strong sexual interest in children. Some of this shows today in the statues, depicting what Americans would regard as perversions, that surround many of India's temples. These shrines used to be centers of child prostitution and tour guides offer numerous explanations as to why the statues are there. Some tell tourists the statues portray the sins for which people come to the temple to be forgiven. Others say the statues remind worshipers what thoughts should be cleansed from their minds before entering the temple, an interesting rationale that should delight the heart of the modern-day pornographer.

During World War II, Bombay's notorious Sister Street displayed both young boy and girl prostitutes in hanging cages, much like animals. The tourist could walk down the street and examine any of the captives; poke them and prod them to his heart's content. Once the tourist made his choice and a monetary arrangement was worked out with the "owner," the subject would be released from the cage and taken to a small, sleazy room. Anything, no matter how perverse, could be demanded and had to be provided if the price was right. The boys, ranging in age from nine to thirteen, would be required to service as many as one hundred men a day. Street urchins were also knowledgeable and would lead customers at night to nearby football fields, large dark arenas often crowded with copulating couples.

Today, in other Middle East countries, boys can be found either in clandestine houses of prostitution or working the streets. Thailand, Cambodia, and Vietnam are all noted for their unabashed activity in the boy business. In Saigon, boys of all ages work as "basket-boys." They hang around supermarkets and shopping centers watching for the unattached adult male to finish his shopping. When he is ready to leave, the boys swoop down, offering to carry the basket of groceries to his home for a few pieces of change. Once they get there, they openly solicit the customer for sex play, usually offering active oral sex. Once a deal has been made, they invariably return to the adult's home the same evening, hoping to be re-hired for a repeat performance.

Factual data about the Orient is so scattered as to warrant only surmise, though homosexuality was known throughout the Orient in ancient and modern times. Ancient Chinese literature contains many descriptions of males making love to boys. There is an interesting difference between Chinese and Greek tastes: whereas the latter preferred masculine, athletic boys, the former preferred effeminate, heavily-made-up boys trained to a degree of perfection. Dennis Drew and Jonathan Drake, in their book *Boys for Sale*, described it this way:

"The boys in the brothels were nearly all Chinese, purchased when quite young, from their parents or from kidnappers. Both parents and kidnappers were rarely prosecuted as long as they paid off the right officials.

"White European children and an occasional Malay were to be found in . . . any fair-sized Chinese brothel . . . even a Negro boy was found in a Shanghai 'house.' For that matter, Shanghai brothels had the reputation of being able to furnish anything a customer could request . . . any age, any sex and any act.

"After World War I, there were a good many white Russian children in these brothels . . . mostly orphans who were lost or abandoned as infants. Probably the children being offered as 'French' or 'German' were actually Russian or, just as easily, the offspring of European sailors who frequented white prostitutes in the seaports."

The book also tells of an English sailor who found an eleven-year-old English boy in a Canton brothel. His wrists had been chained behind his back for two years because he was "disobedient" whenever he was unchained. The boy told the sailor he was chained because he'd protested against the misery of being raped twenty or thirty times a night.

South of the U.S. border, towns of Mexico rival Calcutta and Bombay in the availability of young boys. Indeed, a magazine published every year and called *Gay Mexico*, is dedicated to "all gay Norteamericanos who trip south of the border, and to all of those fabulous Mexican boys who keep them happy." The magazine chapters include "Making it in Mazatlan," "The Action in Acapulco," and "Puerta Vallarta, a Pick-up Paradise." While the magazine itself deals mostly with the adventures and private love affairs of its author, its sales pitch is that it lists the towns in Mexico where the action is. The author comments on being propositioned by two young shoeshine boys and adds:

"Yes, if you're a pedopheliac [sic], you can find plenty of available little kids in Mexico, too!"

Two groups operating out of Los Angeles are apparently finding a ready market for young Mexican boys by operating a round-robin delivery service. One or two adults will drive to any one of the California-Mexico border towns and recruit four youngsters for a trip to Los Angeles. Before leaving Mexico, the boys are scrubbed clean and dressed in nearly-new clothes to make them look as Mexican-American as possible. Getting them across the border into the United States is a comparatively simple matter as evidenced by the fact that California now houses close to a million illegal aliens.

Once the boys arrive in Los Angeles, they are distributed to anxiously-waiting customers. When they have made the circuit, they are driven back to Mexico and replaced by fresh recruits. Police files show that one Los Angeles schoolteacher spent a considerable amount of time bringing groups of boys, aged seven through thirteen, across the border every three months, using the city Hermosillo as his source. He has since discontinued the operation and voluntarily entered a private institution for treatment.

As in the countries of the Orient, abject poverty is the key to, and money is the medium of, the Mexican market. A Tucson man said, "I make regular weekend trips into Mexico and I know that in any town or in any village it's just a matter of selection. Shoeshine boys, newspaper boys, the boys that wash your car . . . any of them are readily available." He added: "I assume that there's a lot of it [prostitution] going on because every boy I've had has done it before . . . with an American."

As in Saigon, Beirut, Calcutta, Mexico City, and other major cities around the world, the "gamines" of Colombia gather in droves outside nightclubs, hotels, tourist centers—brash, street-wise, and aggressive. They'll carry your packages, wash your car, shine your shoes, all the time clamoring for small change. They're also ready to steal anything portable that can be carried at a fast run and later sold. As in other cities, including those of the United States, these boys are the product of a population explosion, a high unemployment rate, and a hopeless future. In Bogota, Colombia, an estimated 10,000 children of all ages live on the streets, hustling by day, and hopefully finding some kind of shelter at night. The world's poverty centers become an international harem for the traveling pederast. The ultimate dream of these street urchins is that someday they'll meet a rich tourist who will like them enough to take them out of their life of squalor and into another world with some kind of security. Some of them do. Most of them don't.

In Europe, one Londoner said: "I go to Spain as often as I can because of the wide variety of available boys, and I've met some beauties. I can sense that some of them desperately want a permanent relationship and there's many a boy I would have loved to bring back to England on a permanent basis. But there's too much red tape and too many questions from officialdom to contend with."

He recounts one occasion on which he was trying to agree to a price for two young brothers he met on the beach. When an acceptable arrangement was made, one of the boys scurried off and returned in a few moments accompanied by his mother. Before the Englishman could fully recover from the shock of parental confrontation, the mother calmly negotiated the figure for complete use of the boys for a two-week period.

*Boys for Sale* tells of a German government official asking a Spanish police chief why something wasn't being done about the swarms of boys on the beach offering themselves to tourists, who were calmly making their selections. The police chief replied it was impossible to prevent a crime when 100 percent of the population was either engaged in it or profiting from it in some way. Besides, as far as the law goes, Spain is probably one of the more permissive countries in Europe. As long as the boy consents, especially with the full knowledge of his parents, there is very little interference from the police, although policemen demanding payoffs from tourists are not unknown. Across the Straits of Gibraltar, in Algeria and Morocco, the pickings are just as easy, particularly in tourist centers such as Casablanca and Marrakech. I asked one tourist how he determined which boys would be available and how he approached them. He replied, "I just pick anyone on the street I find attractive and proposition him." He added that in five vacations in Marrakech, he'd never been turned down.

The Philippines have long been considered happy hunting grounds. In Manila, the boys are known as "bini boys," and enter prostitution at a very early age. The Malayan's combination of tolerance for sexual variety, coupled with the Mideast customs brought in by the Mohammedans, have created an atmosphere conducive to boy prostitution. Bini boys are featured in movies, plays, television shows, and even in newspaper comic strips.

Hotels in Puerto Rico have taken to advertising in gay newspapers in the United States, the ads usually showing a well-built youth, nude, lying in a hammock. Several Puerto Rican kids hustling in New York said they learned their trade in Puerto Rico before coming to the United States. They were attracted to the mainland, they said, by reports of higher prices for their services.

In the United States, there is plenty of evidence to prove that boys were available on the streets of New York in its earlier day. Milton Rugoff offers a great deal of information in his study of sexuality in Victorian America called *Prudery and Passion.*

Rugoff describes an Italian *padroni* of the 1880's who managed bands of boys and girls that begged in the streets. The padroni also set up brothels in which girls of ten and twelve were the main attraction.

Rugoff says: "When the crusading Reverend Parkhurst insisted on seeing something worse than ordinary houses of prostitution, his detective guide took him to the Golden Rule Pleasure Club on West Third Street. The visitors were shown into a basement divided into cubicles in each of which sat a youth with his face painted [who had] the airs of a young girl, a high falsetto voice, and a girl's name. When the guide whispered to the Reverend Parkhurst what the boys did, the clergyman fled in horror."

Rugoff adds that there were similar establishments in other parts of the city.

San Francisco got off to an early start in the boy business, also in the late 1800's, during the Gold Rush. These were the days of the infamous "peg-houses," a name derived from a Mideast custom in which boys were required to sit on greased wooden pegs to dilate their anuses. The customers would be able to see the diameter of the inserted peg and thereby select a boy of suitable dimensions. *Boys for Sale* relates that most of the San Francisco boys were runaways who had traveled West in search of adventure. "They were easily preyed upon and seduced by wily agents who received anywhere from $100 to $500 for each boy they delivered to the brothel syndicate."

During the same period, a homosexual brothel in London offered young postal messengers for sale. It was patronized by those in the highest echelons of Victorian Society—indeed by some from Buckingham Palace itself. After police raided the Cleveland Street brothel, jailing the two men who ran it, a series of cover-ups was instigated to protect the client—cover-ups that rivaled Watergate.

The story didn't come to light until March, 1975, when British officials made public seven boxes of documents that showed how the Victorian establishment closed ranks to protect its noblemen, including knights of the realm. The papers show that Prince Albert Victor, Duke of Clarence, was intimately involved. He was the black sheep of Queen Victoria's family, and may also, it is believed by some modern writers, have been the notorious murderer Jack the Ripper. Lord Arthur Somerset, the equerry to Edward, Prince of Wales, was so deeply involved that he had to flee the country to escape prosecution, despite efforts by Edward (Queen Victoria's eldest son) to protect him. Edward, who was later to become King Edward VII, personally took part in the cover-up, while Lord Salisbury, the Prime Minister, and two other government ministers pleaded with the police and the attorney general to keep the matter quiet. The police were determined to prosecute Lord Arthur, but their efforts were blocked. By the time a warrant was issued for his arrest Lord Arthur, acting on the advice of the Prime Minister, had exiled himself to France. "In such a case as this," wrote one prosecution official, "one never knows what might be said."

One never does indeed. There were surely sighs of relief among the London gentry when the threat of scandal finally subsided. The high moral tone of Victorian society had been saved! But one must wonder if the Cleveland Street scandal—and its attendant horrors—was on this judge's mind when, less than ten years later, he sentenced Oscar Wilde to jail for committing sodomy.

The judge said: ". . . the crime of which you have been convicted is so bad that one has to put stern restraint upon one's self to protect one's self from describing, in language which I would rather not use, the sentiments which rise to the breast of every man of honour who has heard the details of these two terrible trials . . .

"It is no use for me to address you. People who can do these things must be dead to all sense of shame, and one cannot hope to produce any effect upon them. I shall, under the circumstances, be expected to pass the severest sentence the law allows. In my judgement it is totally inadequate for such a case as this."

Just prior to Wilde's sentencing, Lord Arthur had returned to England to attend the funeral of a relative. It was hinted it would be better if he didn't stay too long.

On September 22, 1975, a Central Criminal judge in London called for a cleanup in London's West End as he gave what he called "deterrent" sentences in the trial of a "rent-a-boy" vice racket at an amusement arcade in Piccadilly Circus.

Judge Alan King-Hamilton, at the Old Bailey, sentenced Charles Hornby, a thirty-six-year-old underwriter for Lloyd's of London and four other men, who were part of the racket, to between two and a half to six and a half years in jail for gross indecency and conspiring to procure indecent acts, saying, "As long as you are at liberty, no boy is safe." Young, penniless boys who ran away from home had been attracted to the amusement arcade, the court was told, and then became easy prey for men who offered them meals and shelter.

The name of the amusement arcade was *Playland.*

# 7

# Pornography One

*"The parents of the boys
have already suffered enough."*

As Scott checks his appointment book and Jimmy throws another quarter into a pinball machine, another type of boy prostitute waits patiently for the phone to ring or watches for the mailman. Many of the boys, particularly the older ones, are now using the Madison Avenue approach to advertise their wares in the classified-ad sections of certain newspapers. The ads, usually listed under "Personal Services" offer massage in the home, photographic modeling (also in the home), and personal demonstrations of sex toys. Also included among the ads are some from adults looking for action with the very young.

Apparently this form of advertising works because a new magazine called *Boy Gay-Zette* has appeared in the adult bookstores. It is nothing but classified ads—from every state in the Union plus Puerto Rico and Canada. Some ads include a small picture of the advertiser together with a brief description of his needs and the inevitable post-office box number to contact. There are some obvious incongruities in the makeup of the book. Only some of the photographs are positioned so as to indicate to which ad they refer. Other pictures are just thrown in at random; they are the same pictures of nude boys seen in many of the nationally distributed "chicken" magazines.

*Boy Gay-Zette* is given an international flavor by the inclusion of ads from Australia, Spain, Germany, France, and South Africa to mention just a few of the countries listed. There is no way of knowing how many of the ads are genuine, how many are rip-off artists, and how many have been placed by police departments developing leads.

There have been several attempts to establish "boy-by-mail" operations on a large scale. One such operation was uncovered following the mass murders in Houston. Indeed, it was a suspected connection with the Houston murders (later proved incorrect) that shut down the Odyssey Foundation in Dallas before it really got started. Here's the way Odyssey was supposed to have worked:

Sponsors, selected from a master list of 50,000 prospects, were invited to join the Foundation for an enrollment fee of fifteen dollars. For an additional three dollars, they were sent a booklet called "Fellows 1973," which was a catalog of photos and mini-biographies of hundreds of available boys. Foundation literature explained in decorous terms that Odyssey would arrange for sponsors to meet any of these young men should they so desire: "At a surprisingly modest cost ($20 to $40 a day plus air fare), a sponsor may expedite a fellow's planned program and gain the opportunity to share the adventure." There is no indication of how many "adventures" were shared before the walls of Odyssey came crashing down.

The Odyssey foundation was owned and operated by forty-five-year-old John Paul Norman, a former musician and TV-commercial producer, whose prior police record showed two arrests in Houston for child molesting and sodomy. Young men were solicited to join Norman's organization through ads in homosexual publications or by direct recruitment from the groups of runaways hanging out at Greyhound and Trailways bus depots. Norman's downfall came about because of a complaint by Charles Brisendine.

Brisendine, then twenty-one, had replied to one of the published ads and was invited, by a sponsor, to Dallas. When he arrived, he spent the night at Norman's apartment. They had sex together. Norman explained his operation to Brisendine, still maintaining the façade of a "help" operation. But Brisendine wasn't so easily taken in. It was obvious to him that Norman was setting up a procurement service and many of the young men who would serve as "Fellows" were going to be lured to Dallas under false pretenses. When Brisendine started to go through Odyssey's literature, he found that several of the "Fellows" were missing and information pertaining to them had been stamped "Kill."

This shook up Brisendine. At that time the horrors of the Houston murders were making headlines around the world and Brisendine recounted that Norman had been on the phone continually to Houston and seemed irritated whenever the subject of the Houston murders came up. Brisendine became convinced that Odyssey, somehow, was connected with the Houston murders. He phoned the gay newspaper, the *Advocate*, in Los Angeles for advice. The *Advocate* put Brisendine in touch with their Dallas correspondent, Rob Shivers.

Although Shivers doubted that Odyssey was connected with the Houston murders, he advised Brisendine (after several interviews) to go to the FBI. The FBI apparently felt the same way, telling Shivers that the word "Kill" on the literature was a printer's term that meant the information was no longer to be used.

However, as a matter of routine, the FBI sent a memo to the Dallas police on August 13, a memo that a police-department spokesman said "got quicker attention than most routine matters because of the Houston thing."

The next day, police raided Norman's Cole Avenue apartment and filled a pickup truck with his files containing sex literature, photoengraving equipment, cameras, stationery, typewriters, and hundreds of booklets with names and addresses. A substantial number of these names and addresses had been obtained by answering personal ads in newspapers and magazines similar to those mentioned earlier.

In the investigation that followed, police discovered that John Paul Norman had operated for years in Southern California under the name "John Norman." His post-office-box operation was located in San Diego, and was also known by the name of the "Norman Foundation" and "Epic International." The Dallas police investigation revealed that Norman had a long list of prior arrests and convictions for sex acts with children, although he himself told the *Advocate*, "I've been married twice and got three kids," and then added, "I like variety in bed . . . you name it."

Norman's predilection for variety finally caught up with him. While free on bond in Dallas, awaiting trial on the Odyssey Foundation charges, he fled to Illinois where, a couple of months later, he was arrested in the small town of Homewood and charged with sexual abuse in connection with a group of boys ranging in age from nine to thirteen. He still faces the Texas charges, if and when he shows up there again. At the time of his Dallas arrest, Norman was reportedly trying to set up operations similar to the Dallas scheme in New York and Florida.

During the initial stages of their investigation, Dallas police thought they'd discovered a link between Norman and Houston's Dean Corll. It was merely coincidence. Dean Corll had, indeed, as the record shows, mentioned a homosexual club in Dallas to one of his young accomplices, but there was nothing to indicate it was Norman's organization. In Los Angeles, police checked to see if there was any connection between the Odyssey operation and porno movies being produced in Los Angeles because, a police-department spokesman said, they had information that several of the young boys used in the homosexual films were brought to California from Texas, probably the Dallas area. But while there didn't prove to be any connection with the boys from Odyssey, the check developed a new element.

Some scenes of one movie were shot—in part—on a lonely stretch of beach finally identified as Padre Island Seashore, a new national park extending eastward from Corpus Christi, Texas (about a four-hour drive from Houston). The question was whether the Los Angeles film-makers had gone to Texas to shoot the film there, using local boys (unlikely), or whether there was another group in Texas—unknown to law enforcement officials—who were producing movies.

There was, as we shall see, another group operating in Houston at that time, but they wouldn't be discovered until later. What the investigation did turn up was an internationally-known pornographer with the unlikely name of Guy Strait (probably not his real name). The Los Angeles police had long known about the work of fifty-four-year old Strait. He was self-described as a veritable institution in male nude photography, mail-order magazine publishing, and the gay rights movements of the sixties. He began his publishing business in San Francisco with a gay newspaper called *Cruise News and World Report* . . . an ambitious title that immediately attracted the interest—and the displeasure—of *U. S. News and World Report*. They leaned on Strait and forced him to stop publication. He promptly went into the magazine business and started making a considerable amount of money with what might well have been the first of the commercial chicken magazines: *Hombre, Chico,* and *Naked Boyhood* were among the titles. At the same time, Strait launched a mail-order operation called DOM STUDIOS to sell the magazines, movies, and sets of photographs. Just what "DOM" stands for is a matter of debate. Police officials say it stands for

Dirty Old Man, but Strait claims DOM stands for *Dominus*, the Latin word for "Lord."

Once the DOM studio was rolling, Strait teamed up with another leading photographer in the chicken literary business, Billy Byars, thirty-eight, of Houston. One must assume that Mr. Byars was in the business strictly for art's sake or whatever other fringe benefits there might have been. It certainly wasn't for the money, since Mr. Byars is one of the heirs to the Humble Oil Company fortune.

Byars was shooting kid porno under the title of Lyric International and, when he teamed up with Strait, the joint venture became known as DOM-LYRIC. As one of their magazines describes it, "The art of male nude photography reached a zenith under the aegis of these two artistic persons never equalled—before or since."

At one time, Strait and his associates were reported to have ninety different magazines on the market retailing for five dollars each and wholesaling for two and a half dollars apiece. Distribution lists taken in police raids show the first printing of each magazine was ten thousand copies followed by additional printing runs. The revenue taken in by this group alone was close to a quarter of a million tax-free dollars!

It was the combination of the Houston mass murders and the discovery of Odyssey Foundation that led to the downfall of Messrs. Strait and Byars. Los Angeles police moved in a series of raids. Strait was arrested and charged with contributing to the delinquency of minors, as well as a multiplicity of related charges. As soon as the heat was on, Byars fled to Europe to avoid prosecution. He is presumably there today and will probably stay, since there are at least four outstanding felony warrants for his arrest in this country.

As soon as Strait posted bond, he too left the country for the safety of Europe. An interview in one of Strait's own magazines states: "We have no idea where he is today. . . . Wherever he is—and reliable sources say he is in Turkey or Greece—we wish him well. It is America's loss as his brain is active and intelligent and his interests were much in accord with a large number of Americans who believe that youth is beauty!"

Police officials say, however, that the magazine's emphasis on Strait's being out of the country is a plant; a red herring. He is believed to be back in the U.S., operating out of New York. The three-page interview with Strait, in which he expounds on the art and the inherent beauty of youth, is offset somewhat by the magazine's layout. The youth and beauty sections are juxtaposed with full-page pictures of young boys around thirteen years of age engaged in group anal intercourse.

There is substantial information to show that Mr. Strait's interest in youth transcends beauty. A file in the Los Angeles District Attorney's office suggests that Strait operated a male brothel for little boys in Miami. Apparently boys were being shipped there from the San Francisco area. (An associate of Strait was in the business of selling counterfeit currency and airline tickets purchased with stolen credit cards.)

Strait's group of pornographers was responsible for developing the "stars" in the chicken pornography business. A magazine called *Chicken Little* featured Bobby Moller who was, at the time of publication, eight years old. Parks Earnhardt, an associate of Strait, was busted for his involvement with young Bobby and served some time in the pen while the youngster was sent to a foster home in Southern California. One of Bill Byars's best sellers, *Genesis Children,* portrayed the "delights" of Guy Sommers, a boy whom Earnhardt had imported from Hawaii, while Peter, a thirteen-year-old and one of Byars's favorites, still commands a high price in the chicken market.

Houston police officers were tracing a stolen bicycle in March, 1975, when they accidentally stumbled on a warehouse full of homosexual literature, obscene photographs, and movie film of young men and boys. As their investigation got under way, the officers seized fifteen thousand color slides of boys in homosexual acts, over one thousand magazines and paperback books, and a thousand reels of film. Police said the boys in the photographs ranged in age from eight or nine to the late teens. As the process of identification progressed, police officers discovered several things. First, the ring had been in operation for a long time, since many of the boys in the pictures and magazines were now adults still living in Houston; second, the names as well as the photographs of some of the boys had been passed to the purchasers; and third, there were strong indications that eleven of the boys in the pictures were among the twenty-seven victims of the Houston mass murders. A juvenile officer said they had elected not to develop that aspect of the case because, "the parents of the boys have already suffered enough; there would be problems of positive identification; and we had the leader of the porno ring anyway."

The leader was Roy Ames, who was arrested along with four other men, all of whom were charged with child abuse and jailed in lieu of $150,000 bond. Police said Ames had a prior record of child abuse and that he operated mail outlets in Beverly Hills and San Francisco for the distribution of literature sold through his firm, New Atlas Distributors. New Atlas is still in operation, advertising regularly, in underground newspapers, items geared toward the chicken market. Ames was charged, convicted, and sentenced to ten years in a federal prison to be followed by twenty years' probation on his release. He told officers that, while Guy Strait had worked with him, Strait was small-time by Ames's standards, and that his own material was distributed worldwide.

The Houston raid triggered another round of cooperation between the Houston and Los Angeles police departments, since some of the children in the photographs found in the Houston raid were identified as being from California. It was

the Los Angeles police who discovered—from distribution figures taken in raids—that a significant amount of pornographic
material was being sold to boys' homes and similar institutions
in many states.

But Ames, Byars, and Strait are by no means the only pro-
ducers and distributors of chicken pornography in the United
States. One company in New York is currently offering a discount package on their wares . . . twenty-eight different books
for one hundred dollars; books which normally retail for around
six dollars each. The titles include: *The Pick-up, Paul, Nick,
Barry, Boy Pin-ups, Boys and Men, 200 Boys, Boy Studies, The
Scrapbook of Boys, Boys Together, Kids, Playtime Pals,* and
*Rascals.* Many of the boys featured in these books are young
Cuban refugees from the Miami area and young Puerto Ricans
photographed in New York.

Most of the chicken magazines rely on free-lance photographers for their input and, as might be expected, plagiarism
runs high. One magazine ran a feature on how to photograph
nude boys, what equipment to use, and how to process film at
home. In the copy, the magazine said that at top production it
was processing four thousand pictures a week on equipment
costing less than four hundred dollars. It added that with its
new equipment, it is now producing up to fourteen thousand
pictures per week. Obviously, this doesn't refer to fourteen
thousand pictures of fourteen thousand different boys per week.
Even big-business pornography isn't quite that big. But, even
so, chicken porno is a wide-open market for the adult with a
camera and the kids to photograph.

An example of where all these pictures came from turned
up in Santa Clara, California, when police there arrested a
local high-school teacher and a free-lance photographer running a porno picture ring which, police say, may have involved
250 different adolescent boys over a ten-year period. Over
10,000 pictures were confiscated in the raid and thirty-five-year-

old Roger Ray Murray admitted to police officers that he had already destroyed at least four times the number of photos recovered. Murray's photographic assignments included taking pictures for high-school yearbooks. He was charged with three counts of lewd and lascivious conduct and two counts of sex perversion. Murray received a considerable amount of help and advice from Nathaniel McCray, a thirty-five-year-old science teacher at Graham Junior High School in Mountain View. At least one of the boy participants, a thirteen-year-old, had gone to McCray for counseling at the junior high school. McCray was indicted on three counts of lewd and lascivious conduct with children under fourteen and one count of sodomy, since the police had decided to concentrate their charges on incidents involving boys fourteen and under. Two other adults, arrested in the same raid, were charged with similar offenses.

Most of the boys were identified as being fatherless. According to juvenile officer, Sergeant Tom Hensley, "the boys didn't want to talk about it at first, but when they did, they all agreed they had gone into it voluntarily."

The story broke when a teen-age student went to Murray's apartment with a friend and watched a photography session. He refused to take part himself, went home and told his parents, and they, in turn, called the police.

Murray told the police officers that he had started in the porno business when he was a teen-ager and had an affair with a sixteen-year-old buddy. Murray then started photographing high-school athletes with good physiques, nude. He would photograph young boys at play around town, show them the finished prints, and then ask them to come into the studio so he could take more pictures. From that point on, he would lead them into posing nude singly, then with their friends. The end result was an impressive number of pictures of teen-agers performing homosexual acts, many of them with adults, including those arrested.

But the McCrays and the Murrays and the hundreds of other boy photographers around the country are amateurs, although Murray told the police that he planned to assemble his best pictures for a magazine. "Free Press" newspapers often carry ads in their personal sections from "chicken-lovers" offering to share their collection of pictures with each other on a one-to-one basis. There is no way of determining how many photographs of nude boys crisscross the country in this manner.

Usually a photographer is busted because of his connection with a pornographer. A magazine catches the attention of the police, the distributor is located and arrested, and the distribution lists seized. The lead to the photographer is then usually quite simple. But in a Chicago case, the lead to the photographer came directly from a pornographer who became incensed about the photographic material. Frank Grenard, an investigative reporter for the CBS radio station, WBBM, tells it this way:

"The photographer had an unusual approach. He would talk women, usually unwed mothers or divorcees, into posing for nude shots and—after a few weeks and several sessions—would then talk them into posing for sadomasochistic pictures. If he found out they had children, he would persuade the mothers to bring in their kids for the same treatment. The children were usually around ten years of age or less. The photographer would go through the same cycle with the kids: nude shots first, then the sadomasochistic shots.

"One of the porn kings in Chicago got his hands on the pictures involving the kids, got mad, and called the police."

Grenard recounts that the police vice squad turned the matter over to "C-5," an undercover police investigating unit and one of their agents started buying pictures from the photographer. After a few weeks, the police, armed with a search warrant, busted the photographer's Diversey Avenue studio and seized about half a million pictures and a full set of sadomasochistic paraphernalia. Half of the pictures seized were of nude children on torture devices. Grenard recounts that the porno distributor said, "I can go along with a lot of things, but this fucking shit is trash and I'll do anything I can to get guys that do this kinda crap!"

# 8

# Pornography Two

*"It must be stimulating
the hell out of someone."*

Hard-core pornography is not hard to find, although some legal restrictions have been placed on its publication and distribution. In 1970, the President's Commission on Obscenity and Pornography reported that gross sales of sexually-oriented material amounted to over 2.5 billion dollars. Indeed, the Commission's report itself became, overnight, a pornographic best seller when an entrepreneur took the report in its entirety and reprinted it—official cover included—with sex photographs added to "illustrate" what the Commission was talking about. The book enjoyed brisk sales until the long arm of the law brought the enterprise to a close.

The official report of the President's Commission dealt with general-release films, stag movies, art films, sexually-oriented mass-market books, and various under-the-counter sex photos, gadgets, and toys. The Commission reported that 85 percent of adult men and 70 percent of adult women had been exposed to such material, most of it on a voluntary basis. Furthermore, it reported that about the same 85-70 percentage of boys and girls had seen "visual depictions" or read "textual descriptions" of sexual intercourse by the time they were eighteen. The study also reported that adult bookstore operators said most of their customers were "predominantly white, middle-class, middle-aged, married men."

The Commission found that while the majority of American adults feel they should be permitted to read or see any sexual materials they wish, they also feel that young persons should be prohibited access to some sexual materials. As we know now, the suggestions made in the Commission's report were ignored by then-President Richard Nixon and, late in 1973, by the Supreme Court. The Court returned the issue to the individual states which had the authority to ban any work which, taken as a whole, was sexually prurient or offensive and was without any "serious literary, artistic, political or scientific value." It was a decision that created a great deal of chaos.

But a discussion of the pros and cons of pornography is not within the scope of this book. The question here is whether exposure to pornography, and participation in the production of pornography, is leading the youth of America down the road to depravity and contributing to the increase in sex crimes.

One recently completed research project strongly indicates that not only are fears of pornographic influence groundless but that some exposure to pornography may actually be salutary. The report, for example, found that a sample of rapists had seen less pornography as teen-agers than had a comparable group of normal adults. The same was true for child molesters. Steady customers of an adult bookstore had also seen less erotica than the control group used in the study. These findings grew out of research studies done for the Commission on Obscenity and Pornography by the Legal and Behavioral Institute. The researchers were H. S. Kant and M. J. Goldstein who collaborated with psychiatrist Lewis Judd, of the University of California at San Diego and Richard Green, of the University of California at Los Angeles. The purpose of the study was to determine if a relationship existed between experience with pornography and the development of normal or abnormal sexual behavior.

For the study they used sixty deviants—recently admitted patients at the Atascadero State Hospital in California. They were Caucasian males, each of whom was either charged with, or convicted of, rape or molesting children. The child molesters were separated into two groups, those who used boys as sex objects and those who used girls. They also selected fifty-two users of pornography who were customers of an adult bookstore in Los Angeles.

For the control group, the UCLA research center selected sixty-three Caucasian males from the Los Angeles area whose ages and educational backgrounds matched those of the sex offenders.

A trained interviewer spent two hours with each person, questioning him on 276 items that covered demographics, sex attitudes, sex history, fantasies, and exposure and reaction to pornographic books, photographs, movies, and live shows. The questioning followed systematic order, starting with the most probable stimulus (sadomasochistic activity). The subject was asked to recall the number of times he had seen each type of stimulus during his adolescence, and also during the year prior to the interview.

Most respondents had seen examples of partial nudity as teen-agers; few had seen examples of sadomasochistic activity. In general, rapists and child molesters had seen less pornography of all kinds than those in the control group. The rapists differed less from the control group than did the two groups of child molesters but with significant differences: rapists were much less likely than the normal group to have seen representations of fully nude women, of normal intercourse, of oral-genital contact, or of sadomasochistic activity.

The child molesters had seen less pornography of every kind than had the normal group. Only 62 percent of the sex offenders who preferred children had seen representations of heterosexual sex acts, while 85 percent of the control group had encountered this kind of pornography as teen-agers.

The avid buyers of pornography showed a pattern closer to the deviant samples than to the normal group. As teen-agers they had seen less pornography of every kind than did normals. It appeared to the researchers that sex deviates were markedly lacking in adolescent experience with stimuli that represented culture's definition of a "normal" sex act.

During the year before they were confined, the sex offenders had seen less pornography than controls had. The gap between rapists and normals was more striking in later years than it had been during adolescence, especially for photographs and films of heterosexual intercourse, male nudity, and oral-genital relations. Child molesters who chose boys as sex objects had seen less heterosexual stimuli than normals had, but about the same amount of homosexual pornography as the normals had seen. Child molesters who chose girls had seen less pornography of every kind than had normals. In short, adults in the control group had seen more pornography when they were teen-agers, and had seen it even more often as adults, than had the sex criminals.

But while the UCLA study is impressive in both its scope and its content, and while it was conducted by some of the leading experts in the country, it is at odds with opinions from some equally qualified experts and people working in the juvenile field on a daily basis.

In Richard Kyle-Keith's book, *The High Price of Pornography*, Dr. George W. Henry, Professor of Clinical Psychiatry at Cornell University College of Medicine, says he feels the increase in sex crimes and the various forms of deviation are, to a substantial degree, the result of reading pornography. Dr. Henry believes that: "... the majority of people are so constituted and live in environments such that they will grow up to be reasonably normal in their sexual adjustment. There is, however, quite a large proportion of the population who are susceptible to such training as may be obtained from these publications, and whether or not they arrive at a point of violence is perhaps an academic matter in view of the other problem—that no one can tell ahead of time who is going to arrive at that goal once they have been exposed to these publications. Furthermore, there are all degrees of sadism and masochism which enter into human relations and which seldom get into the newspapers.

"The reasonable assumption that pornography creates sexual deviation is inescapable. Since a statistically undeterminable, but probably very large, number of persons turn to sexual deviation if an opportunity offers itself, it is likely that the reading of smut constitutes a sizable training ground."

Dr. Henry points out that there is some confusion in the public's mind about the meaning of "children," and "adolescents." He suggests that when people use the word "children," they mean "adolescent," and "everyone knows that the adolescent is most sexually excitable, and has the least legitimate opportunity to find an outlet for that sexual excitablity. As the result of that they find every conceivable means of finding an outlet. . . . It is an error also to assume that if you sell something to an adult it doesn't get to an adolescent. A great many of these so-called adults are really still adolescents, and feel most at home with actual adolescents. More than that, some of them are primarily interested in introducing adolescents into abnormal practices."

In the same book, Dr. Benjamin Karpman, Chief Psychotherapist at St. Elizabeth's Hospital, in Washington, D.C., noted that "there is a definite relationship between juvenile delinquency and sex life. . . . Our life from our point of view is guided by our instincts. We have two main instincts. The self-preservation instinct, and the race-preservative instinct, commonly known as the hunger and sex instincts."

Dr. Karpman adds: "Instincts spread by tension—you and I will never know that we are hungry unless there would develop in the stomach some sort of tension which sends a message to the brain and tells us that we are hungry. In other words we know of our sex life and of our personal life, of hunger life, only through the medium of tension developing.

"Tension is tension. When a younger boy . . . is reaching adolescence, he is hungry for information about sex, but for some reason or other he doesn't get it at home because the mother and father are too tired to talk.

"Where is the boy going to find it [release from tension]? He cannot find it at home. He doesn't always find it at school. Very few schools have developed to the point of giving lectures on the subjects of the facts of life. He looks for it in the gutter, and there he comes across pornographic material and literature, and that draws him into all sorts of gang life, which discharges itself as juvenile delinquency. If he cannot discharge it in a sexual way, he discharges it in a criminal antisocial way."

The Chief Neuro-Psychiatrist and Medical Director of the Philadelphia Municipal Court, Dr. Nicholas G. Frignito, whose position affords an unusual opportunity to evaluate the effects of obscenity and pornography on the conduct of youthful law violators, contends that antisocial, delinquent, and criminal activity frequently results from sexual stimulation creating such a demand for expression that gratification by vicarious means follows. "Girls run away from their homes and become entangled in prostitution. Boys and young men who have difficulty resisting the undue sexual stimulation become sexually aggressive and generally incorrigible. The more vicious delinquent or psychopathic type may become an exhibitionist, a rapist, a sadist, a fetishist. He may commit such antisocial acts as arson, pyromania, or kleptomania, which are often symbolic sexual acts.

"The Philadelphia Municipal Court," according to Dr. Frignito, "has case histories in which sexual arousal from smutty books led to criminal behavior from vicious assaults to homicide. Some of these children did not transgress sexually until they read suggestive stories and viewed lewd pictures in licentious magazines. In several instances these children were very young, varying in age from nine to fourteen years. The filthy ideas implanted in their immature minds impelled them to crime.

"Sexual stimulation by printed material does not always lead to crime, but it is always an inducement to impurity and in the more suggestible leads to aberrant forms of sexual misconduct, incest, voyeurism, and narcissism.

"Our prisons, correctional institutions, and mental hospitals are jammed with many of the unfortunates who were prey to pornography. Many never recover their mental or physical health. Others may never have freedom.

"Pornography is an instrument for delinquency, it is an insidious threat to moral, mental, and physical health. It debases the true meaning and function of sex, and it incites to immoral and antisocial activity.

"The purveyor of pornography is an immoral, corrupt, degenerate individual who completely disregards the harm he causes to public morality and decency."

"Sergeant Don Smith, a pornography expert with the Administrative Vice section of the Los Angeles Police Department exclaimed, "In every single case we've worked involving young boys . . . and that's more than I care to think about, we have found hard-core pornography in every home we've raided. We've seized films, books, and photographs by the ton. Since the pornographic market is a billion-dollar business in California alone . . . it must be stimulating the hell out of someone."

But while there is disagreement among the experts on the effect of pornography on the young, there is no disagreement that pornography is a booming business providing millions of dollars to its purveyors. One thing is certain, however: none of the boys lured into posing, performing, or recruiting others into the porno business has gotten rich. The boys report they usually get somewhere from fifteen to twenty dollars for each session plus other inducements such as booze, drugs, clothes, sex, and the "kick" of doing it.

There is another area in the chicken-literary business that deserves attention: the paperback book. These are not under-the-counter books. They're readily available by the hundreds in any adult bookstore. *Chicken Chaser, Wynter's Tail, Jock Stud, Buddy's Butt, Do it . . . Son, Fun After School, Door to Door Chicken, Meat My Buddy, The Child Watchers, A Boy for Hire, Boy Nymphet, Boys for Dessert* are just a few of the titles.

The publishers in this precarious business apparently feel their salvation lies in conforming to the Supreme Court's comments. Thus, they try to endow their books with "serious literary, artistic value."

The foreword to one of these books asks: "What does a chicken cruiser—one who is horny, hearty, good-looking, well-educated and stuck in a small east coast town—do to change his life for the better? He goes to work at a boy's boarding school, of course, and lets it all hang out."

The book is then described as "a frank, descriptive novel of a man who needs boys and the boys who respond to that need. . . . On a deeper level," it continues, "it is a story about human relationships and the love on which they are founded."

The publisher apparently feels it is in his best interest to shift the focus of his book from the level of hard-core pornography to that of literary excellence. To do this he equates his book with outstanding literary successes. After pointing out that sex between males—many under age—isn't shocking to civilized minds anymore, he adds: "In 1948 Gore Vidal published his epoch-making *The City and the Pillar,* in which for almost the first time in American fiction, a boy's love for another boy was described with the dignity it deserves."

The publisher then assures the reader that the forthcoming erotic scenes grow out of the deep feelings the book's hero and his boys have for one another and "are not just used to arouse mechanically the lurid interest of the reader." He sternly points out that the book is a serious novel and "it is our expectation that you will be deeply moved by it."

Another paperback, *Male Incest*, is described as "the moving story of a young man who discovers that his father and older brother are having an affair. After trying his luck in San Francisco, he returns home and becomes a real member of the family."

Yet another paperback deals with the adventures of a teacher at a boarding school for boys between the ages of nine and fourteen. The writer apparently decides to give a Tennyson-like quality to a description of what it is about boys that appeals to men. After a page of glowing prose, he gives up and gets back to porn-writer basics. His protagonist, the teacher, has just completed a round of sexual gymnastics with Ronnie, his twelve-year-old favorite who, lying naked on his stomach, asks his teacher: "You said you liked my body. What exactly do you like about it?"

The teacher replies, "I like the way your hair hangs down over your right eye. I like your right eye. I like your left eye. I like your hair because it's so silky. I like the shape of your head, how it goes out here and then curves inward. I like this little point of hair at the nape of your neck. I like your nose and your slightly flared nostrils, and your mouth—the way it curves—and your long neck, and how this vein stands out. And I like your chest, and especially your proud little nipples that get hard when I rub them like this. I love your belly, because it's so nice and flat, and your belly button because it's yours. And I love to feel these bones—your hipbones—and I like these two lines leading to your thing, making a V, as if pointing the way; and I love your thing, which seems to be getting hard again. And I love these two things in their sac, and how they jump around when I squeeze them like two peas in a pod. And I love your thighs, so smooth and fine, and your knees, and especially this hollow behind them. And I love your sturdy legs, so firmly shaped, and your feet, like Picasso's circus boys'. And then I love to run my hand down your straight spine like this, counting the vertebrae. And I love these two dimples on either side, right above your behind and then finally, I love this part . . . these two round perfectly shaped hemispheres, your buttocks, your nates, your posterior, your backside, your rear end."

"In other words," Ronnie responds, "you like my body o.k., but what you really dig is my ass!"

But the most significant book on the market is not a porno book at all, but a thirty-two page travel guide, published in 1972, called *Where the Young Ones Are*. It contains listings of 378 places in fifty-nine cities in thirty-four states where ". . . the young can be found." In the preface of the book, which is printed on cheap, colored mimeograph paper stapled together, it says: "We have tried through representatives throughout the country to provide an accurate listing of where the young action is today. All listings have been checked and verified. However, the possibility of error does exist due to human interpretation of such words as 'young,' 'active' and the like."

Having copped out on that, the writer then adds what is referred to as "a message of caution": "The age of consent varies between state and state. Check your state and the states you travel through for the current status. Also many communities have numerous ordinances for loitering, curfew violations, and other activities you may engage in. Protect yourself and the person you would be with." He then adds a final cautionary "Although many times you are morally right, you can be legally wrong. Stay happy and free to enjoy 'Where the Young Ones Are.'"

The recommended places to find "action" with young boys include amusement arcades, beaches, parks, certain street corners and parking lots, roller- and ice-skating rinks, bowling alleys, YMCA's, miniature golf courses, movie houses, sand dunes, pool halls, book stores, and boys' clubs. One town even has its high school listed.

A spot check revealed that many of the locations were correctly listed and there was, indeed, hustling going on. But whether the listings were accurate or not is really academic. Since the book contains no salacious material and no photographs, its obvious that 70,000 people spent five dollars apiece just to find out where the young ones were. There would be no other reason whatsoever for buying the book. And that's quite an audience—for any book.

# 9

# Violence in the Gay World

*"How can anyone seriously ask why children are violent?"*

In March, 1974, the editors of *Esquire* magazine addressed themselves to the question: "Do Americans Suddenly Hate Kids?" Eleven top writers were commissioned to express their points of view. The subsequent articles included such subjects as "How to Disown Your Child," "How to Store Your Child," "The High Cost of Childhood," "On the Rage of Black Children," and "The Fate of the Boys Next Door," the last of which dealt with the Houston mass murders.

The problems, and the desirability of child-rearing were, to say the least, starkly depicted and made a convincing argument for not having children. The overall message was that American family life as portrayed by television's "Father Knows Best" and "Dennis the Menace" was long since gone, if indeed it ever existed in the first place.

Of course men and women continue to produce babies, and are able to survive their upbringing. But the inescapable facts so well explored in *Esquire* remain: that an increasing number of parents regard their children as burdens; that there is an expanding population of parents who are either neglectful or hateful or vicious; and that a frightening percentage of American children are being subjected to enormous abuse.

Reports of atrocities to children are manifold and sorrowful. Summaries of news stories that were published in California during a twenty-day period provide startling testimony.

In Port Hueneme, a two-year-old boy died of head injuries after he had been taken to Ventura County General Hospital by his uncle and a female companion. They told the attending doctor the child had been injured in a fall down a flight of stairs. Following a thorough examination of the body, the two were arrested on suspicion of murder.

In San Bernadino, a father was booked on suspicion of murder. A spokesman for the County Sheriff's office said at least three witnesses told officers they had seen the man toss a boy's body over an embankment on Highway 330. According to the Sheriff's office, the man's five-month-old son had been fatally beaten a few hours before his body was found.

In San Francisco, an eighteen-year-old mother and her twenty-year-old boyfriend were taken into custody after they brought her two-year-old son to a hospital. The child was in a coma and covered with bruises. He died later of a lacerated liver. The girl told police she and her boyfriend had spanked the baby because he had wet the bed.

In Los Angeles, two infants were found abandoned within a thirteen-hour span. Three teen-agers discovered a newborn boy in a paper sack thrown on a front lawn, while Archie Edwards, a refuse collector, saved a newborn girl who had been relegated to a trash can. Both of the abandoned babies were estimated to be about two hours old.

Ms. Donna Stone, founder of the National Committee for Prevention of Child Abuse, says: "Our statistics indicate that more than 60,000 children [in the United States] die each year from child abuse. There are at least two deaths a week in New

York City and the Los Angeles Police Department has said murders resulting from the abuse or neglect of children have increased 53.5 percent since 1965." Ms. Stone adds: ". . . we think the reported statistics are only the tip of the iceberg." Donna Stone includes, in her statistics, deliberate starvation, sexual abuse, gross neglect, and psychological torment. In the general category of child abuse, she says, "Abuse is the major killer of children under two and [intentional] neglect occurs ten times as often as abuse—and is much more difficult to get at. You don't see the emotional injuries."

Boy hookers are often the products of homes in which they have been victims of child abuse or neglect. Frequently, after they have begun to seek affection, independence, and safety on the streets, their troubles are compounded when their parents discover their activities. The parents' reaction is almost inevitably violent. A case in point is related by Father Jack McGinnis of Houston:

"Manuel came to First Step when he was eleven. He had been in Harris County Youth Village three times since he was ten. He had a long string of delinquent behavior, much of it before he was ten years old. He was impossible in the Village; he would not adjust at all. The officials there asked me if I would take him and I did. He lived with me for a year and was a fine boy. A real character, but really sick. We had him tested and the psychiatrist told me that 'he's one of two or three percent for whom we predict no change whatsoever. He's severely sociopathic.' I said 'Baloney, we'll see about that.'

"One of the most tragic experiences Manuel had was when his father got so enraged while drinking that he threw the boy completely through a sheetrock wall of their garage. This is only one of many such examples of how the boy was treated by his parents. At eleven, Manuel hallucinated his father coming to beat and kill him. He'd scream at night. This was, very clearly, where his severe and deep alienation began. The experience left very, very deep mental wounds and scars. I'd say ninety-nine percent of his behavior was just a wild expression of all that had happened to him, directly related to how mean and cruel his father had been.

"Manuel stayed with us for a year and never once ran away. He couldn't function in school, so I tutored him at home. I really loved him and he loved me. Gradually, he began to change. We never talked much about things he did, and I never got on him about things. We used discipline—not punishment. There were certain types of behavior we would tolerate and others we didn't. But the only form of discipline we'd use was to have Manuel stay in a room for a while or take away his lesser privileges. We never touched him physically—never spanked him or paddled him or anything. We never dared touch him. And that's what they constantly did to him at Harris County. They paid no attention to the fact that his father had beat hell out of him for years. They had a system and it said that if you're bad you get paddled. And so they paddled him and he'd run away and steal something. He functioned just beautifully with us after a while. He was really getting somewhere.

"Unfortunately we had to close because we were in a bad location, the funds weren't coming in, and we were having various other problems. Manuel had to go home. He stayed there about six months before he got into it again with his father and started down the trail to the Gatesville, Texas reformatory. When Manuel was in Houston, he hustled on the streets for money. He was very popular in the gay neighborhoods. And he was well paid.

"I talked to Manuel about seven or eight months ago. He's eighteen years old. He said he was not gay, nor was he interested in gay activities at this point in his life. He had a girlfriend and was actively involved in heterosexual experiences. Why did he hustle? A lot of times because he'd be walking along the streets thumbing a ride and somebody would pick him up, be nice to him, and proposition him. That happened to him quite a bit.

"Well, Manuel's in prison now. He's doing three years for

drug abuse, possession of dangerous controlled substances. He's in a prison that's not doing a thing for him but putting him in solitary when he won't work. It's just making him more bitter and more angry. Nobody along the way tried to find out, to substitute or supply the intimate relationship that would touch the roots of his alienation. The whole system has failed him."

NYPD's Sergeant William McCarthy also speaks harshly of parental attitudes: "It [violence] stems from the general attitude of the families we deal with. When we tell the parents or guardians what their little darlings are into, some of them couldn't care less—and those that get angry get angry for all the wrong reasons. The fathers get mad because they see their [son's] sexual deviation in terms of black and white. When we tell them their son has been hustling, they feel the kid's deviation is a direct reflection on their own masculinity. Their immediate reaction is to beat the hell out of the kid to 'make a man' of him." McCarthy brooded thoughtfully, "Some societies use witchcraft; some use voodoo. In the United States we use violence."

Beatings, however, rarely "make a man"; they usually drive the boy further away from that which might bring him self-respect and fulfillment. Chickens, like other troubled children, seldom find the understanding and guidance that would encourage them to master their fears, to deal with their pain, to seek their measure of happiness. They are, instead, subjected to further mistreatment that is, in many cases, doled out by publicly supported institutions; institutions that are supposed to be "rehabilitating" them. Society faces a new breed of child . . . the FAAC, the Furiously Angry American Child. But this is not a new breed to those who work with juveniles on a daily basis. Doctor Scott C. Guth is an assistant Professor of Psychiatry at Tufts' New England Medical Center and Director of Alcoholism Services at the North Central Massachusetts Mental Health Center. Guth said he was amazed at the number of young addicts he had treated who were selling their bodies to acquire drugs. In an interview with the *New York Times*, he sketched a gloomy picture of the life-style of many American youngsters:

"On the one hand, I am presented with reports of atrocious and cruel treatment of children every day. These reports come to me from children when they feel safe from parental retribution, and from their parents, the perpetrators of the cruelty, during the course of treatment.

"On the other hand, I read of the great public perplexity of 'experts' who are struggling to develop theoretical concepts to explain the ever-increasing cultural violence and anger of America.

"Could it be television violence or is it 'permissiveness' in child-rearing that causes the outrageous acts, the furious behavior of our youth?

"For the sake of intellectual integrity as well as for developing policies of remediation, it must be recognized that many American children are furiously angry and that their anger must be determined by their life experiences. I can expect to hear that their fathers worked very hard all their lives and often held two full-time jobs. They were always very tired and drank a lot. Mothers usually held full-time jobs, and the children were taken care of by siblings three or four years older, literally from infancy. Many children in middle America are taken care of by other children.

"If there is 'permissiveness' in child-rearing in our country, it is all too often attributable to the virtual absence of parents as nurturing adults in the lives of their children. In this context of permissiveness, because parents are absent most of the time, the most horrendous cruelty is exercised toward children.

"Recollections of how mother and father used to get drunk on Christmas Eve are very common. It was after a vicious brawl with drunken father that mother locked herself and five children, under ten, in the kitchen and turned on the gas in a maca-bre ritual of preparation for a better life than this 'God-damned hell.'

"A five-year-old child was ordered to kneel on dried split peas scattered on a hard wood floor. When she collapsed be-cause that incredibly painful posture could not be maintained, she was whipped viciously with a leather belt. Beatings of chil-dren with horsehair whips; drunken, raging fathers holding pis-tols to the heads of their sons; children hurled bodily against walls are virtually commonplace clinical histories.

"Mothers and fathers weep as they recall the terror they ex-perienced in their own childhood. They continue to weep with remorse and guilt as they tell me of their inability to prevent their awful rage from breaking bounds and terrorizing their children.

"How can anyone seriously ask why children in America are violent toward the things and people in their surroundings? A much more plausible question for behavioral scientists must be: 'How can the level of retaliatory rage children accumulate in American society be so minimal in its expression as violence?'

"I am impressed by the ability of children to absorb and be guided by the value stance of their parents and the culture, which prohibits retaliatory anger. Even so, as a clinician, I ob-serve that these children tremble, wet the bed, fail at school, think they're different from other people, and hate themselves for being so awfully fearful and angry.

"Some will begin to steal, set fires, and torture animals. Most will continue to follow the submissive, terrified humiliation that is the lot of children in our society when they are possessed of angry parents. But when they begin to feel strong enough to take the risk, the rage that is proportionate and appropriate to their experience of abuse, exploitation and torture will emerge almost as surely as a falling body obeys Newton's law."

Guth asks, "Why can't their anger be acknowledged? Who

is being served by the obfuscation of the causes of their anger? Why is it so difficult to look squarely at the horror millions of Americans—most of whom, but not all of whom, are alcoholics—are visiting on their children every day."

It is easy to document incidents of violence in the gay world. There was, of course, Houston, where at least twenty-seven young boys were tortured and killed.

More recently, in August, 1975, police in St. Louis held five teen-agers, including a fourteen-year-old boy and an eighteen-year-old girl, for the slayings of two boys who were sexually assaulted, beaten with heavy frying pans, mutilated with a knife, and stuffed into a sewer. Police said the victims, one fourteen, the other sixteen, were accosted by the teen-age gang who'd been "popping pills and smoking grass."

That same week, four men abducted a twelve-year-old boy in Los Angeles and drove him across the country, forcing him to commit sex acts with them on the way. They told the boy they were taking him to Chicago where he was to be sold for sexual purposes. They were arrested in Fenton, Missouri, when they were stopped for speeding.

A sixteen-year-old boy from Pennsylvania had just arrived in San Francisco. He was picked up by two men near San Francisco City College and driven down the peninsula to a spot about twenty-five miles south of the city, spread-eagled in the back of a station wagon, and castrated. Within a matter of hours, sheriff's deputies arrested two suspects, an eighteen-year-old short-order cook and a telephone-company repairman, age thirty-four. In their station wagon was a set of surgical instruments—and the boy's testicles. Both men said they were homosexual. The older man worked as a counselor for the Helping Hands Community Center, a gay organization.

In Scranton, Pennsylvania, a man on parole from a mental institution (even though he had confessed to killing his great-aunt) was held for the "sex-murders" of two thirteen-year-old boys. About 200 people pelted him with snowballs when he was escorted from the courthouse after being arraigned.

In Philadelphia, twenty-eight-year-old Sanford Shore was convicted of second-degree murder in the stabbing death of a fourteen-year-old boy whom he had picked up hitchhiking. He testified he told the boy there was a bomb in the car and he would blow him up if he didn't do as he was told. Shore then said he bound the boy with a necktie and "remembers being on top of him with a knife in my hand and there was blood on it."

Twelve years before, the City of Brotherly Love started a program for delinquent boys as a result of a scandal in which a sixteen-year-old boy from a good family murdered a fourteen-year-old boy he met in a movie theater. The older boy invited the younger to his home on the pretext of showing him his chemistry set. When the younger boy rebuffed the elder's sexual advances, he was stabbed thirty times and left trussed up behind the garage.

In Rochester, New York, a seventeen-year-old was found guilty in the stabbing assault of a fifty-six-year-old man the boy had known since he was eleven. The youth claimed he was defending himself against homosexual advances by the older man ... a former social worker. The boy testified he had stabbed the man in an attempt to prevent him from committing an act of sodomy. In court, the man denied he was a homosexual. In any case, the jury was unimpressed with the boy's evidence. The prosecutor argued that the boy, who had known the man for six years, went to his apartment willingly, knew what to expect, and made no attempt to escape.

Stories of violence like these are commonplace and the emergent picture is that of the gay world as a bad scene; that homosexuals are prone to violence. There is absolutely no evidence to support this. Indeed, a lengthy study undertaken by the Institute for Sex Research (ISR) in Indiana found that homosexual offenders against children almost never used force, but that heterosexual offenders against children often did. The study also found that in the case of homosexuals, half the time they were friends of their child partners, and in half the cases resolved in court, the boys had actually encouraged the offenders. This suggests that cases in which the boy is the instigator occur much more frequently than those that end up in court.

The Institute's study was based on interviews with over 1,500 men convicted of a wide variety of sex offenses. The authors of the study concluded that the claim that homosexuals are prone to violence is a myth; that violence seems to be a prerogative of heterosexuals.

A San Francisco psychiatrist, Dr. Martin Hoffman, makes the following comments in his book *The Gay World*.

"It is a matter of empirical fact that the consenting adult homosexual who gets in trouble with the law is *not* prone to commit violent crimes or crimes against children. Homosexuals are no more prone to seduce young boys than are heterosexual males to seduce young girls."

In referring to the ISR's study, Hoffman offers a theory as to why force or violence would not be a factor in a sex relationship between an adult male and a young boy:

"In 45 percent of the cases, masturbation was the technique, and in 38 percent of the cases, fellatio was performed on the boy. Anal intercourse occurred in only 4 percent of the cases. [Hoffman does not explain the unaccounted 13 percent.] Masturbation or fellation of a boy involves producing an erection on his part and bringing him to orgasm. I think it is not difficult to see that this can only be done with the cooperation of the boy. In other words, these sexual techniques are not susceptible to force or violence. One cannot bring a boy to orgasm unless he is a consenting partner."

Hoffman emphasizes that the exclusive male homosexual

is not the characteristic sex offender against children: "He is much more likely to be a man who has been, or will be, married and who also has a tendency to want sex relations with young girls." He concludes, ". . . the suggestion, made by police officials, that the consenting adult homosexual who is arrested is a potential danger to children or is prone to violence is simply not true."

What is true is that those boys convicted of this type of crime almost inevitably meet a new adversary: the American juvenile justice system.

*Chapter*

# 10

# The Institutional Fallacy

*". . . 109 different victims and*
*276 different aggressors. . . ."*

While the lot of the child plagued with
an unhappy home life is not a pleasant one, it is often mild
when compared to the life of one who enters the juvenile justice
system. Now his life will be controlled by juvenile authorities,
the juvenile "experts," the professionals. Unlike the brutal parent, who is sometimes arrested and convicted for his actions,
the professional almost never is because everything he does—
every action he takes—is always in "the best interest of the
child."

Take a look at the case of Danny Crossland, sketched by
Mike Royko in the *Chicago Daily News*, in July, 1974. Fifteen-
year-old Danny was, at the time, clinging to life in a Chicago
hospital after overdosing on drugs. Columnist Royko became
interested in the case and checked into Danny's background.

As Royko angrily put it: "It's hard to believe that one kid's
life could be so thoroughly botched up by people who are being
paid to know what they're doing." According to Royko, Danny,
at the age of eleven, had been taken out of a snake-pit family life

by a Chicago Juvenile Court judge. For several years Danny was shuffled from institution to institution, from foster home to foster home, and was even sent out of the state to a private children's home in Texas. (Illinois, at that time, and for some peculiar reason, was shipping a number of its dependent and neglected wards to homes in Texas. The plan finally fell through when it was learned the Texas facilities were, at best, "shoddy" and Illinois brought its kids back to their home state.)

Danny finally ended up at a state-run temporary home called Edwards Center, where kids were kept until something better could be found for them. According to Royko, Edwards Center was a disgrace. The superintendent didn't believe in locked doors. Kids ran away at will and had easy access to drugs.

Danny, like many others, ran away several times, was returned by the police, and would just as promptly run again. There was another series of transfers and another series of running. He was then placed in a program called "Outreach," which, Royko said, should have been called "dumping ground." Under this program, the state moved Danny into the Lawson YMCA, paid his rent and food bills, gave him fifteen dollars a week . . . and complete freedom.

Royko pointed out that the Lawson Y is one of Chicago's most popular homosexual hangouts, located in "the heart of a thriving vice, drug, prostitution, boozing, you-name-it-somebody's-got-it area." Danny roamed the streets at will and got involved in acid, speed, heavy drinking, and the world of sex. He was not yet fifteen. When the police found him, he was near death from an overdose.

Royko summed up bitterly, claiming that Danny was properly the ward of the state. That meant the state was supposed to take the place of his parents . . . and if real parents had done what the state did to Danny, a judge would have thrown the book at them.

Later, Royko said in a phone conversation that Danny survived the drug overdose. But one wonders just what this experience has done to Danny's mind. It is extremely unlikely that he will develop into a normal, well-rounded human being. He is a product of the state; an individual manufactured by society. Later in life, society probably will have to face Danny Crossland, and thousands like him, again.

Dr. Richard Korn, with the School of Criminology at the University of California, read this statement made by a San Quentin prisoner to the Subcommittee to Investigate Juvenile Delinquency:

"In my lifetime, I have murdered twenty-one human beings, committed thousands of burglaries, robberies, larcenies, arsons and last, but not least, I have committed sodomy on more than a thousand male human beings. For all these things I am not the least bit sorry. I have no conscience, so that doesn't worry me. I don't believe in man, God nor the Devil. I hate the whole damn human race including myself. If you, or anyone else, will take the trouble and have the intelligence or patience to follow and examine every one of my crimes, you will find that I have consistently followed one idea through all of my life. I preyed upon the weak, the harmless, and the unsuspecting. This lesson I was taught by others; might makes right."

In spite of the overwhelming mass of evidence illuminating the failures of the juvenile justice system, it continues to stagger along. Judge Lois G. Forer of Philadelphia told the same Subcommittee to Investigate Juvenile Delinquency:

"I regret to report to you that, with a few notable exceptions, we are failing; we are failing to give our young people an understanding of the importance of the rule of law in a democratic society; we are failing to educate our young people to live in a highly technological, complex, and difficult world; we are failing to provide them with the skills they need to make an honest living in a society which places so much emphasis on financial success and material possessions; we are failing to give them the medical care and treatment necessary so that they may grow up to be physically and emotionally healthy adults; we are failing to give them a sense of compassion, kindliness, and love toward other people because we do not treat our young people with compassion, decency, and love."

The theory behind institutionalization is that if a boy cannot learn to live within society's rules, then he must be locked up so that society is protected from him—all this done, of course, in the best interest of the child.

The sheer madness of the theory must surely be obvious. Put in simplistic terms the cycle is as follows: A boy is having a problem in school. The parents go to the juvenile authorities and complain they can no longer handle the boy and ask for help; they have given up. Even if there are alternatives, the parents rarely know what they are. So the hapless parents and the helpless boy stand before a juvenile judge, often unqualified, who sets the judicial process in motion by bringing the boy into the juvenile-justice pipeline—that grim, inept system so stoutly supported by the grim, inept people who administer it.

Once in the juvenile-justice maze, the boy joins the half million other children being held annually in juvenile facilities, many of them for such "crimes" as truancy, talking back, petty theft, running away, and a litany of other inconsequential incidents that have been foisted off on the public as juvenile crimes. The boy will be thrown into contact with others committed for murder, rape, arson, drug abuse, drug dealing, burglary, mayhem, and manslaughter.

Dr. Korn put it this way: "We persist in these activities in the face of incontrovertible evidence that we are failing. Even so, this failure does not result in the loss of our exclusive confession, our monopoly we defend against all competition, especially from private citizens. Our field is almost unique in that failure is a virtual guarantee of greater prestige, power—and more money. I can think of no other business in which the failure of the product has been so successfully used as an argument for more of the same operations that produced it. . . . In spite of all the trouble we take, and all the suffering we inflict, the security and peace of the citizenry—who are the victims of crime—continues in jeopardy. And that jeopardy appears to be growing."

There was a case in Philadelphia, in 1968, that clearly illustrates just what institutional life is like. An attorney complained to the court that his client, a slightly-built youth, had been repeatedly raped by some prisoners while they were all being transported in the sheriff's van. Just a few weeks later, the same attorney, Joseph E. Alessandroni, again filed a complaint that another of his clients, whom the judge had committed to the Philadelphia Detention Center merely for pre-sentence evaluation, had been sexually assaulted within minutes of his admission.

The judge ordered an investigation and, at the same time, Frank L. Rizzo, who was then Police Commissioner, started a parallel inquiry of his own. The two investigations, which were later merged, revealed that sexual assaults in the Philadelphia prison system were epidemic.

As prison officials admitted, virtually every slightly-built young man committed by the courts was sexually approached within a day or two of his admission to prison. Many of those young men were repeatedly raped by gangs of inmates, while others, because of the threat of gang rape, sought protection by entering into a homosexual relationship with an individual tormentor. Only the tougher and more hardened young men, and those few so obviously frail that they were immediately isolated for their own protection, escaped homosexual rape. After a young man had been raped, he was marked as a sexual victim for the duration of his confinement. The mark followed him from institution to institution. Many of these same young men were released back into their communities full of shame and full of hatred.

That was then, and is now, the sexual system that exists not only in Philadelphia prisons but in prisons and juvenile institutions across the country. It is a system that imposes a punishment that is not, and could not be, included in the sentence of the court. Indeed, it is a system under which the least-hardened criminals, and many men later found to be innocent, suffer most.

Let us trace the ordeal of one young man as described to Senator Birch Bayh's Subcommittee to Investigate Juvenile Delinquency. "I was assigned to 'E' dorm. Right after the light went out, I saw this colored male, Cheyenne; I think his last name was Boone. He went over and was talking to this kid and slapped him in the face with a belt. The kid was saying, 'I don't want to.' After being slapped with the belt, he walked back with Cheyenne and another colored fellow named Horse. They were walking him back into 'E' dorm. They were telling him to put his hand down and stop crying so the guard wouldn't know what was going on. I looked up a couple of times. They had the kid on the floor. About twelve fellows took turns with him. This went on for about two hours. After this, he [the kid] came back to his bed and he was crying. He stated that 'They all took turns on me. They all took turns on me.' He laid there for about twenty minutes. Cheyenne came over to the kid's bed and pulled his hands down and got on top of him and raped him again. When he got down, Horse did it again and then about four or five others got on him. While one of the young guys was on him, raping him, Horse came over and said, 'Open you mouth and suck on this and don't bite it.' He then put his penis in the kid's mouth and made him suck on it. The kid was hollering that he was gaggin' and Horse stated, 'You better not bite it or I'll kick your teeth out.' While they had this kid, they also had a kid named William in another section of 'E' dorm. He had his pants off and was bent over and they were taking turns on him. This was Horse, Cheyenne, and about seven other colored fellows. Two of the seven were brothers. Horse came back and stated, 'Boy, I got two virgins in one night. Maybe I should make it three.' At this time he was standing over me. I stated, 'What are you looking at?' And he said, 'We'll save him for tomorrow night.'"

During the twenty-six-month period examined by the Philadelphia study group, they found there had been 156 sexual assaults that could be documented and substantiated through institutional records, polygraph examinations, and other corroborative devices. Seven assaults took place in the sheriff's vans on the way to or from the prisons; 149 in the institutions themselves. Of the sexual assaults, eighty-two consisted of buggery, nineteen of fellatio, fifty-five of attempted and coercive solicitations to commit sexual acts. There were 109 different victims and 276 different aggressors. The report concluded that for various reasons the figures were undoubtedly much higher.

In their investigation of sexual assaults, the Philadelphia study group excluded any cases of truly "consensual" homosexuality. Nonetheless, they said, it was hard to separate consensual homosexuality from rape since many continuing, isolated homosexual liaisons originated from a gang-rape or from the ever-present threat of gang-rape. Similarly, many individual homosexual acts were possible only because of the fear-charged atmosphere. This threat of rape, expressed or implied, might prompt an already-fearful young man to submit. Prison officials, these studies stated, are too quick to label such activities "consensual."

At the opposite end of the spectrum from innocent victims

of homosexual rape are the male prostitutes. The homosexuals, known as "sissies," "freaks," or "girls," were supposed to be segregated from the general prison population. They were, however, readily available. The study group learned of repeated incidents in which homosexual "security" cells were left unguarded by a staff that was too small, or too indifferent, or turned their backs so that certain favored inmates could have sexual relations. Many of these male prostitutes were created not only by force, or the threat of force, but by bribery. In prison life the definition of "prostitution" must be expanded to include motives of self-preservation. An inmate may prostitute himself in order to assure himself of protection. In such situations economic gain may not be the best kind. Typically, an experienced inmate will give an inexperienced inmate cigarettes, candy, sedatives, stainless-steel razor blades, or extra food pilfered from the kitchen. After a few days the veteran will demand repayment in sexual terms. It is also typical for a veteran to entice a young boy into gambling, have him roll up large debts, and then tell the youth to "pay or fuck." An initial sex act then stamps the victim as a "punk boy" and he is pressed into prostitution for the remainder of his imprisonment.

The study group said they were struck by the fact that the typical sexual aggressor does not consider himself to be a homosexual or even to have engaged in homosexual acts. This attitude—prevalent nationwide—seems to be based upon a startlingly primitive view of sexual relationships, one that defines as male whichever partner is aggressive, and as female whichever partner is passive.

The Philadelphia system is, unfortunately, typical of others across the country. One youth told about an incident he witnessed in a New York facility. "A boy was caught in a homosexual act. They kicked in his head with steel-toed boots, took all his clothes from him, and, in the middle of winter (and it gets like two or three or four below zero) they poured cold water on the floor, took all the furniture out of the room, locked it, and made the boy sleep on the floor and the water with the window open."

In testimony given to the Subcommittee to Investigate Juvenile Delinquency in late 1971, Joseph Rowan, Executive Director of the John Howard Association in Chicago (a prestigious organization that deals with the problems of released and incarcerated prisoners), complied to a request from Senator Bayh, who had asked the organization to file a follow-up report to previous testimony given the committee by Patrick Murphy, who was at that time the Chief Attorney of the Juvenile Office of the Legal Aid Bureau of Chicago. In nearly all cases the John Howard Association supported Murphy's claims. In one particularly interesting instance they disagreed: that relating to consenting homosexual behavior between two juveniles. This report also sketches the horrors of juvenile institutional life.

"Mr. Murphy states that he recently filed civil-right suits on behalf of 'two thirteen-year-old boys who were caught in consenting homosexual behavior in Elgin State Hospital. These two boys were placed in restraints for 72½ consecutive hours as punishment for their conduct.' The institution denies the fact that the boys were placed in their beds for 72½ consecutive hours but rather states they were let up to use the bathroom facilities, to eat, and for some well-supervised recreation. However, they did not deny that the remainder of the time the boys were restrained in their beds. The complete story on this case should be put into a total perspective. First, what is consenting homosexual behavior for juveniles? Certainly, no one would want their child going to an institution knowing that he could fall into 'consenting homosexual behavior.' What is consenting homosexual behavior for an adult should not be interpreted as necessarily being the right thing for juveniles. Mr. Murphy gives the impression that because this was 'consenting' that the children should not have been disciplined. However, if this was the case, then children should have the right to smoke or drink. This is nonsense. Not only do children of this age need protection when they are 'normal' and have an 'average' intellect, but when one considers that these are emotionally disturbed, very likely low-IQ children, more supervision and guidance are needed in making decisions for these children.

"Furthermore, it should be noted that the one child who is described [by Mr. Murphy] as the 'plaything for the ward,' and who is the recipient of homosexual behavior, contracted anal gonorrhea from a young lad who was the aggressor and who had just been home for a weekend furlough where he contracted gonorrhea. The recipient of the homosexual behavior was the 'punk' for the entire ward. Thus, after several children had become involved in the homosexual behavior, it had ended up that within a period of two weeks seventeen of the twenty-three boys on that ward had active cases of gonorrhea. Certainly something should be said for the lack of close supervision. However, even with the best supervision, there are still opportunities for children, particularly emotionally disturbed ones, to get involved in homosexual acting out.

"There are no 'quiet rooms' or 'segregation areas' for children at Elgin State Hospital. Thus, it is felt that restraint must be used if a child is to be kept from interacting with the general population. Children, when restrained to a bed, are given six to eight inches of movement for their arms and legs, even with the restraints. . . . There is no doubt that this does seem to be a 'crude' and almost inhuman way of restraining children. However, this is the only alternative that the hospital felt it had. For many of these children drugs and medication have not proven helpful in restraining them in acting-out behavior."

The John Howard Association report, in its summary, provided a grim warning: "It is not likely that there are many states which have services better than Illinois as child welfare is not a priority in our country today. So long as we put our emphasis on other areas the helping professions will only be 'stepchildren.'"

There is an even more deadly game being played in some boys' homes. The clandestine "selling" of young wards to gain favors from rich patrons or, at times, to get rid of the boys.

One boys' home—privately operated—is in a well-to-do state. It's one of many homes across the country operated by local funds, sometimes with county subsidies. This particular home was formerly a grade school, left vacant when the town's small population started drifting off to the bigger cities. The home provided facilities for pre-delinquents, boys from about ten years of age through sixteen. The average population of the home was forty boys who were "supervised" by a husband-and-wife team aided by some part-time help. The board of directors was composed of local businessmen whose main concern was to keep the home running on a break-even basis. They would rally around when the home's pickup truck broke down or a clothing drive was needed. All the boys attended public schools, but were forced, because of their local "notoriety," to be clannish. Since the home itself was twenty miles out of town, the boys kept pretty much to themselves.

The home provided the bare essentials only: food, shelter, medical attention, clothing . . . and that's all. There was no counseling, no tutoring, and the only structured programs were the chores around the school that provided food for the tables. The ranch's board of directors hoped local citizens would take selected boys into their homes, at least for weekends. But the locals weren't too interested in any such direct support. So life at the school for the boys wasn't grim. It was just dull. Evenings and weekends would be spent just hanging around. The rape of young boys by the older boys was commonplace. When it was discovered, it would be dismissed with a gruff, "Quit that fooling around or you'll slop the hogs for a month."

There were three brothers at the ranch, ages twelve, fourteen and fifteen, the sons of a fundamentalist preacher. They would fall into the so-called "wild-boys" category. Their prime interest, and their major diversion, was sex. The two older boys would often amuse other boys in the dorm by forcing their younger brother to fellate them or to fellate others who had, in turn, become indebted to them. "Force," however, is the wrong word because the younger boy thoroughly enjoyed every available type of sex activity.

These three brothers might be considered lucky. One of the more active fund raisers—and a charter member of the home's board of directors—was the local pediatrician, who was particularly taken with the three brothers. The doctor was married and had two children of his own, but at least one of the brothers would spend the weekend at the doctor's house; often all three would spend the weekend there.

During these periods of contact with the doctor, the brothers would advise him as to which boys at the ranch liked to play around . . . and what specific act they preferred. The doctor had a constant supply of young sex partners literally at his beck and call and even had the three-brother team training them for him.

Several other men—usually single—in the same area would also arrive at the home on Friday evenings to pick up boys of their choice for weekend fun. What was really going on was well known to every boy at the ranch, but the chosen boys were considered very lucky by the others; in a position to be envied. The boys not selected would urge their friends to arrange a weekend for them with their adult partner.

The supervisors of the home presumably were also aware of what was happening, but as long as the adult was presentable and picked "safe" boys, the supervisors went along. There was, of course, no open solicitation. Everyone played the game to everyone else's satisfaction. One particularly attractive boy— much in demand for weekends—claimed he had made it with every other boy in the school by promising to take them with him on his weekend trips.

The ranch is fortunately closed now due to a lack of funds. The pediatrician has lost interest in the two older brothers but still uses the services of the younger boy, who now recruits other boys from the town itself.

Earlier, (on p. 117) you read a bitter statement made by a San Quentin prisoner who has spent most of his life in jail. The quote was from the closing part of his statement. In the opening part, he described his experiences and feelings as a juvenile:

"I started doing time when I was eleven years old and have been doing practically nothing else since then. What time I haven't been in jail, I have spent either getting out or getting in again. What you have done and are doing to me you're also doing to others. What I have done to you many others also do to you. Thus, we do each other as we are done by. I have done as I was taught to do. I am no different from any other. You taught me how to live my life and I have lived as you taught me. If you continue teaching others as you taught me, then you, as well as they, must pay the price and the price is very expensive. You lose your all—even life. Now, you who do not know me or my wishes, you decide without consulting me in any way. I tell you now that the only things you or your kind will ever get from me for your efforts on my behalf is that I wish you all had one neck and that I had my hands around it. I have no desire whatever to reform myself. My only desire is to reform people who try to reform me and I believe that the only way to reform people is to kill them. I may leave here at any time for some big house, mad house or death house but I don't give a damn where they put me. They won't keep me long because no power on earth can keep me alive and in jail for very much longer. I would kind of like to finish writing this whole business in detail before I kick off so that I can explain my side of it even though no one ever hears or reads of it except one man. But one man or a million makes no difference to me. When I am through, I am all through and that settles it with me."

It would be easy to dismiss this as the raving bitterness of a particular individual, but that's too easy. The fact is, he is all too typical a product of our juvenile-justice system. It is inescapable that a large percentage of our adult criminals are also products of our juvenile training schools.

*Chapter*

# 11

# The Educational Fallacy

*"Five hundred and ninety million
dollars a year evaporating in a
cloud of shattered windows
and destroyed equipment."*

There were many misspellings but the message was tragically clear:

*Dear Mom and Dad:*
         *We committed sueaside because wear no good and no longer a part of the family. So, so long from us. Rembrance. Sorry about this.*

This note was left by ten-year-old twin brothers from Pittsburgh, in August, 1975, before attempting to take their own lives by stabbing themselves, taking rat poison, and inhaling ether from an aerosol can. When the boys were found by their mother, one of them still had a knife sticking in his stomach. The two boys were despondent after being scolded by their father and ordered to write "stealing and lying are two commandments that should not be broken" six hundred times. Both boys survived.

In September, 1975, an eighteen-year-old Eagle Scout and honor student from San Diego was sentenced to life imprisonment for the hatchet killings of his parents and older sister. Daniel Alstadt had been disciplined by his father for poor grades. After the killings, young Alstadt set fire to the house and went to a party.

Around the same time, sixteen-year-old Michael Slobodian went on a murder-suicide rampage in Brampton, Ontario, and opened fire at his high-school classmates and teachers. He killed a teacher and a student, wounded thirteen others, and finally turned the gun on himself. His sister said he told her he was "fed up with life" and that he wrote a note to the family saying he was "going to eliminate some people" and kill himself. He was angry, she said, because his English and physics teachers had written his parents asking about his poor attendance.

The number of teen-age suicides in the United States has tripled in the last decade. It now runs at the rate of thirty a day. More than half the patients in the nation's psychiatric hospitals are under twenty-one years of age.

Dr. Darold Treffert, Director of the Winnebago Mental Health Institute in Oshkosh, Wisconsin, places part of the blame for the alarming increase in teen-age suicides on what he calls "the American fairy tale." He says the "fairy tale" has five elements: that more possessions mean more happiness; that a person who produces highly is more important than one who produces less; that everyone must belong to and identify with, some larger group; that perfect mental health means having no problems; and that a person is abnormal unless constantly happy.

"For some," says Treffert, "the American fairy tale ends in suicide or psychiatric hospitals, but for countless others it never ends at all."

He referred to millions of Americans plagued throughout their lives by a gnawing emptiness or meaninglessness, expressed not as a fear of what might happen to them but rather as a fear that nothing will happen to them. Treffert claims Americans must stop evaluating themselves according to what they own or what they have done, and learn to accept and cope with their various mental and emotional problems.

"Parents," he said, "should avoid trying to make their children live up to the standards of the fairy tale and treat them as individuals, as persons, rather than possessions." He added, "We measure our country in terms of gross national product but overlook our gross national neurosis which is our preoccupation with producing."

Obviously, we are not preoccupied with producing stable, well-rounded children when one out of eight Americans is mentally disturbed and the psychiatric industry is doing a roaring business. American children have been shortchanged and there are strong indications they know it. Yet, in spite of the fact that they continually tell us this in dozens of different ways, we continue to ignore the message. We view the rapidly rising rate of delinquent behavior with considerable alarm and demand prompt corrective action. But the "corrective action" usually consists of advocating "get tough" policies. It rarely includes looking at the cause of delinquent behavior.

Child experts to whom we have faithfully listened over the years say they need more money to control juvenile crime. But even when more money is made available, it is invariably spent in the wrong areas. A graphic case in point is the wave of vandalism hitting schools across the country.

Vandalism is now costing the taxpayer over five hundred and ninety million dollars a year. Five hundred and ninety million dollars a year evaporating in a cloud of shattered windows and destroyed equipment! J. Arlen Marsh, editor of a study on school security says, "The cost of replacing broken windows in the average big city would build a new school every year!" This incredible waste of money is often referred to as "senseless." But is it senseless? There's a very strong, clear message there if only we care to listen.

A study called "Urban School Crisis" says that "Students look upon the school as alien territory hostile to their ambitions and hopes, that the education which the system is attempting to provide lacks meaningfulness, that students feel no pride in the edifices in which they spend most of their days."

This vandalism cost equals the total amount spent on textbooks for every school in the country in 1972. But school officials react to the message by spending an equal amount of money on security, not to prevent the vandalism but to arrest those responsible for doing damage.

For example, in 1965 the Los Angeles school system had a total of fifteen security guards. In six short years, apparently without anyone getting the message, that force was increased to over one hundred members at a cost of over a million dollars a year. During the school year 1972 to 1973 that figure was doubled again, with Los Angeles spending over two million dollars for security agents.

In New York, the figures are even worse. In 1971, New York taxpayers laid out $1,300,000 for security guards plus an additional $3,500,000 for police stationed in the schools. In spite of the expenditure, the cost of vandalism for the same period was at least $3,700,000.

These figures are often dismissed as being part of the price of big-city living. But that just doesn't jibe with the facts. Included in the top fifty crime centers in the United States are Phoenix, Daytona Beach, Fresno, and Albuquerque. And those cities are listed in the top ten!

An even greater problem than vandalism is violence in the schools and society's apparent willingness to accept it as a part of everyday school life. Teachers and students are being murdered, assaulted, raped, and robbed in schools at a steadily increasing rate. Between 1970 and 1973, in Dayton, Ohio schools 362 teachers were assaulted; in Kansas City, Missouri, over 250 teachers met the same fate in the same period; in Chicago, a pupil shot and killed his elementary-school principal.

The fact that 70,000 teachers are physically assaulted in school by children every year prompted this entry in a booklet put out by the United Federation of Teachers: "If the student is not armed, a woman should remember that her knee or almost any instrument can become a weapon. A Bic pen will open a beer can or a kidney or an eye."

The booklet also advises, "The surest means of preventing sexual attacks is never to be alone."

Senator Birch Bayh described the statistics of today's school violence as "a ledger of violence . . . that reads like a casualty list from a war zone or a vice-squad annual report." A 1973 survey conducted in only 757 school districts showed that over one hundred students have been murdered in the schools. One urban school district report the confiscation of over 250 weapons—hand guns, shotguns, and rifles included! In Los Angeles, alone, of the 222 students expelled between 1973 and 1974, seventy-six were ousted for the possession of firearms, three times more than in the previous year.

The Los Angeles school-system security force now numbers 300 peace officers, making it the third largest police force in Los Angeles County. In spite of this security, Jerry Halverson, Associate Superintendent for the school district, told of an elementary-school teacher who was accosted in the classroom by an assailant who held a knife to her throat, forced her to strip, and raped her in front of the class.

Halverson, describing the conditions in the schools as "catastrophic," said, "This escalation [of crime in the schools] which could be viewed as analogous to the spread of a destroying cancer, must be stopped before it becomes terminal." He then told the Subcommittee on Juvenile Delinquency that, just as there is no one single cure for all forms of cancer, there is no one cure for the violent and destructive acts going on in the schools.

Educators are understandably alarmed—and rightly so. Violence in the schools is an intolerable situation that concerns everyone and requires immediate, positive corrective action. As Halverson says, there is no single cure. But those being suggested are self-protective; school officials refuse to recognize the fact that the cause of the problem is in the school system itself. Such an admission would acknowledge failure over the years, and professionals in the kid business are not noted for being quite that candid. It is much easier, much safer, and certainly more palatable to blame the students. But modern educators with excellent credentials are not accepting this defensive posture any more.

In 1970, just about the time violence in the schools was starting to escalate, Charles E. Silberman, editor, author, and former college teacher, published *Crisis in the Classroom* after completing a three-and-a-half year study commissioned by the Carnegie Corporation. The book rocked the educational establishment. It was expected that the book would have a major impact on educational debate in the United States. But if there was any debate, there is no indication it had any effect. Instead of making changes, the schools, guided by time-worn principles (and principals), clattered on downhill toward instant disaster. Silberman warned that the schools were preoccupied with order, control, and routine for the sake of routine; that students were essentially subjugated by the schools; that by practice and systematic repression the schools were creating their own discipline problems; and that the schools were promoting docility, passivity, and conformity among the students.

Silberman pointed out that, despite attempts at reform during the late 1950's and early '60's, the curriculum in use throughout the country is often characterized by "banality" and "triviality." To a certain extent, Silberman defended the teachers and attacked the system. He argued that schools are intolerable, not because teachers are incompetent, indifferent, or cruel. "Most of them," he wrote, "are decent, honest, well-intentioned people who are victimized by the current system as much as students are." "The central cause of the problem," he further states, "is that school and teacher-training institutions are afflicted by 'mindlessness': that educators fail to think seriously about the purposes and consequences of what they do, . . . about the relationship of educational means to ends, . . . and that they would seldom question established practices." "In the elementary schools," said Silberman, "much of what is taught is not worth knowing as a child, let alone as an adult."

In June, 1975, two California psychologists, after studying both prisons and high schools, found a frightening parallel between the two institutions. Craig Haney and Philip Zimbardo of Stanford University, in an article prepared for *Psychology Today*, said that American high schools are like prisons "with guards posing as teachers and students learning how to be docile prisoners." They said the teachers, like prison guards, have absolute authority over students and that the teacher's word always counts more than the student's. They reported that students, like prisoners, are regimented and regulated by roll calls, bells, fixed hallway routes, and classes run mechanically for specified periods "regardless of the natural education process."

They added that high-school students, like prisoners, must obey codes of dress and personal comportment.

"Both prisons and high schools" the Stanford researchers said, "feel compelled to limit the length of male inmates' hair, as though long hair were some grievous threat to institutional authority."

They described high-school buildings as "huge, stark and architecturally barren" resembling buildings designed for punishment and incarceration. (Silberman, in *Crisis in the Classroom* similarly described them as "oppressive, grim, and joyless.")

Today's school system has very little to do with education. Rather, it is churning out vast armies of functional illiterates. Parents, employers, and students themselves are finding out that students did not even learn the basic functions of reading and writing.

One California boy discovered he'd been shortchanged by the system when, after graduating from high school, he went to apply for a job. His reading and writing "skills" were so inadequate he was unable to fill out a simple application form. His family promptly filed suit against the school board.

In another case, also involving a California graduate, a boy enlisted in the Air Force but was discharged from basic training due to his inability to read. His family also filed suit. The judge scheduled to hear the latter case warned that school boards across the country could be facing billions of dollars in losses in similar suits. Admittedly, one must wonder where the parents were in these cases if it took them so long to discover their child's shortcomings.

There is, it appears, a direct relationship between the inability to read and the juvenile delinquent. According to judges and juvenile workers, the greater percentage of youngsters involved in delinquent acts are unable to read. A children's court in New York said in a study that non-readers made up over 75 percent of those arrested. A Ford Foundation study also found that the incidence of delinquency is much higher among school dropouts than among those who graduate from high school.

Conditions in California have reached such a point of decline that in January, 1975, three members of the Sacramento School Board announced they were tired of the district's failure to properly educate its students. Board President Grant Bennett warned he may send his children to a private school because of his "lack of confidence in some aspects of the system to meet their [his children's] needs."

California's Governor, Edmund Brown, Jr., sharply criticized the school system while speaking to state Democratic leaders. He emphasized his reluctance to give them more than the 4.6 percent increase he had earmarked for schools in his state budget proposals. Said Brown: "When I see schools that are permeated with violence, boredom, and irrelevance, I think something is wrong." The governor added: "I am committed to learning but I am not committed to pouring more money down this complicated pipeline which I don't understand."

Governor Brown's sister, Kathleen Brown Rice, decided to campaign for the Los Angeles City School Board and won handily. Her platform charged that schools were graduating students who "can't read, write, or qualify for a job." Mrs. Rice called for new priorities in school funding, saying that "school programs must be accountable and must produce results in order to continue being funded."

The devastating combination of boredom and hassle in both school and home sends over a million young runaways each year looking for a better deal. From their point of view, anything they find has to be better than what they have, because most of them have very little.

California does not stand alone with its dismal picture of "education." All across the country parents are beginning to wonder just what they're getting for their educational tax dollar. An NBC documentary revealed that East Coast schools were reporting truancy rates of up to 40 percent. While this figure by no means reflects the national average, it does reflect the national trend. School officials everywhere reluctantly admit that truancy is on the rise. Since there is a correlation between illiteracy and juvenile crime, it is reasonable to assume that the increase in the rate of juvenile delinquency is directly related to the failure of the schools.

The act of running away is invariably preceded by a period of truancy and it is the truant boy, footloose, on the town in the daytime, broke and with nothing to do, who is most vulnerable to the chickenhawk. In Chicago, one chickenhawk said: "In the daytime, I work the cheap movie houses and the amusement arcades. If I see a boy sitting alone in the early afternoon . . . I'll invariably score with him. He's bored and broke and I can solve both those problems for him."

In the major cities, many boys have begun to hustle for the same reasons . . . and in the daytime. They rarely run short of customers.

This is not to suggest that boys are turning to prostitution because of a woefully inadequae school system. The young hustlers represent a very small percentage of the total student population, but the social system, which includes the schools, sets the pattern. A poor home life, a poor school record leading to eventual dropout, the shortage of work, the lack of adult interest, and the lack of money . . . all these, taken collectively, provide the ideal situation for the adult chicken hawk.

School systems are geared to the proposition that every child must have a complete education in order to become the President of the United States ( a laudable ambition that might have declined in the past couple of years ). They ignore the fact that there are children who are not interested in middle-class norms. They ignore the fact that "leaving school" does not necessarily mean dropping out of the educational system completely. They ignore the fact that some children will benefit more from informal learning and vocational training than from a constant academic preparation for college, now the only apparent purpose of formal education. School systems even have the power to force those students who oppose them to toe the line. This enforcement capacity has not only been singularly unsuccessful but has become, albeit unwittingly, a major cause of enforced juvenile delinquency. Dr. Richard Korn described the process to the Subcommittee to Investigate Juvenile Delinquency:

"A young man refuses to go to school. We know that he won't make it in life unless he gets an education. Our objective now is to get him to go to school. He rejects persuasion, so we place him on probation in order to induce him to accept persuasion. But he refuses to see his probation officer. So we place him in an institution, in order to make sure he cannot escape our attempt to give him counseling. But even in the institution he resists seeing his counselor. So our objective now is to force him to see his counselor. But when we come for him in his room, he violently resists and, in order to fulfill our original objective, we must now first subdue him. We can't help him if we are injured ourselves. Our immediate goal, therefore, is to render him incapable of injuring us—using whatever force the situation requires.

"Step by step, from this original plan of 'let's make it in life together,' we get into this particular situation where it is his life or ours. This is the madness of it."

It is interesting to notice that we no longer measure education by quality, but by quantity—much like a prison sentence. Kids are never kept at school because their education hasn't been good enough. In general, once a student is nineteen or twenty he is no longer kept in school. The slow learner drags down the school's overall grade and academic record. If a child can't measure up, he will eventually drop out because the system has very little time, money, or inclination to give much in the way of individual attention. But the term "dropout" was invented by the system itself when, in fact, there are very few dropouts. There are "force-outs" and "kick-outs," kids who become bored and discouraged with school. The school, in turn, becomes bored and discouraged with them because they "have nothing to offer."

If you were to question a panel of teachers, blame would be laid at the feet of the school administration, the parents, and the child . . . in that order. The administration, they would say, doesn't support teachers in their efforts to run a tight class; they are powerless to exercise any type of control and discipline. The parents, teachers charge, are not spending enough time seeing that the child comes to school properly prepared, with his homework completed and with the "correct attitude" to school and authority. The children, teachers claim, have their minds distorted by television, drugs, movies, and the new morality.

While many of these charges may be valid, it is the schools themselves that have become preoccupied with law and order, in many cases merely for the sake of law and order rather than the necessity of it. An excerpt from a national education manual cautions: "Be ready to use the first minutes of class-time. If you get to Johnny right away, he has no time to cook up interesting ideas that do not fit into a class situation. . . ." This might well be good advice, but surely the first requirement of a good teacher is the ability to control a class in all situations and to be able to direct a class in any and all ways.

American education today forces every child to be alike; it forces the school to create a system that subordinates real education to haphazard control; it forces a return to the law of the jungle and has turned many of the nation's schools into armed camps. The resulting pressures are sending many children fleeing to the oblivion of drugs.

*Chapter*

# 12

# The Drug Obsession

*"I never started a kid out
on drugs . . . I don't have to."*

Wayne Henley, a junior-high-school
dropout, woke up from an acrylic-paint stupor in a house in
Pasadena, Texas, a Houston suburb. He found himself handcuffed. Next to him lay a naked fifteen-year-old girl and a
twenty-year-old boy. They were lashed spread-eagled to a
board; their mouths gagged. There was a smell of death in the
air as Dean Corll yelled, "I'm going to kill you all . . . but first I'm
going to have my fun." He was brandishing a .22-caliber pistol
as he raged. Henley later confessed, "I sweet-talked him and
promised I'd help torture and kill them if he'd let me go. Dean
wanted me to screw the girl while he did the boy. . . ." Henley
convinced Corll and was released. A little later Henley had the
gun in his hand and pumped five rounds into Corll's chest.
". . . I felt grotesque. Now I can breathe."

By midnight that same day, law-enforcement officers had
dug up the first eight of twenty-seven bodies of young boys—
most buried in a storage shed rented by Dean Corll. By morning, the grisly details of the Houston mass murders were flashed
around the world.

Houston Police Lieutenant Breck Porter told the press: "This is the type of thing where you have this clown who gets these kids up to his apartment on one pretext or another . . . a party or something of that nature. They get up there and they sniff paint, sniff aerosol, . . . eat pills, and all that dope bit, you know. There's really no violence connected at first . . . just everybody having a good time. They was invited to party and some of them liked it. One of them came back nine times to Corll's place. . . . There was lots to eat, lots to drink, and plenty of pills and marijuana. Then, when they wake up, they find themselves on this board—the old torture-rack type thing—and that's when the sex bit starts."

In the murky world of boy prostitution, drugs are a very big deal. They are used as a medium of exchange, to relax inhibitions, to tempt, and, in some cases, to control. A fifteen-dollar lid of grass or five hits of acid are eagerly accepted in exchange for sexual services. Many of the kids themselves are minor-league dealers and will supply their customers with drugs as well as with their bodies. Most of the murdered boys in Houston were not runaways in the classic sense. They were not from other cities but were local kids, most of them from a neighborhood known as the Heights, an old run-down section of Houston populated by broken families, old people, society's losers, and doped-up kids. The teen-agers lived for drugs, which created the ideal escape from a dull, boring life.

Indeed, drugs were the basic attraction in the Houston murders. Wayne Henley and David Brooks would prowl the streets hustling young kids for Dean Corll. The proposition was always the same: "Let's go up to Dean's for a party." And the not-so-innocent youngster would go along to find that Dean had laid out a tableful of acid, pot, pills, and booze. Whatever they wanted, Dean had it, and the exchange wasn't that hard to take. Except for twenty-seven of them.

At the time of the Houston murders, the "in" drug was

"kwazis," the street name for methaqualone, known commercially as Sopor, Quaalude, Somnafac, Optimil, or Parest. In 1972, methaqualone was the sixth-ranked sleeping pill in America (in terms of sale) until it suddenly developed a quite undeserved reputation as a "love drug," a powerful aphrodisiac. With this discovery, demand for the drug shot up almost overnight and the American pill-manufacturing companies obligingly geared up to meet the new demand. Kwazis quickly appeared in tremendous quantities on high-school and college campuses across the country. Pushers reported that Sopors were outselling everything else at rock festivals. But it turned out that the "heroin for lovers" was not as advertised. Sopors, when used in conjunction with alcohol, would very likely kill. The nation's campuses had become an open testing ground for yet another drug.

Particularly in the major cities, junior and senior high schools—even elementary schools—have become major distribution centers for drugs. Youthful dealers in New York report sales of up to $600 a day to fellow students. A preliminary investigation by the Senate Subcommittee to investigate Juvenile Delinquency shows that drug- and alcohol-related offenses on school property, in the three years between 1970 and 1973, increased by 37.5 percent. Bear in mind that these figures were based on offenses discovered. The actual figures would be much higher and there is every indication the increase between 1973 and 1975 is greater still. A study released in 1975 by the National Educational Association (NEA) estimates that drug-related crimes in schools had increased by 81 percent since 1970 and that a whopping 30 percent of the 18 million students in secondary schools use illegal drugs.

The National Highway Safety Administration estimates that 50 percent of the nation's high-school students go to drinking parties every month and 61 percent of that group gets drunk once a month. The same study also found that these students represent a remarkable cross-section of our school population. "They are not far out, dropout, alienated, or underachieving types. On the contrary, they represent all levels of scholastic achievement and aspiration. They report the same range of sport and extracurricular activities as the students who are not involved with drinking."

Far too many parents, unfortunately, still manage to keep drugs and drinking in separate categories. Indeed, a child getting drunk is generally considered preferable to one getting stoned on marijuana and there is ample evidence to show that the increase in teen-age drinking is due to parental approval of alcohol as a substitute for drugs. It also serves to offset some parental guilt. It's all very well to lecture children sternly on the evils and horrors of marijuana, but a lecture is weakened somewhat when it's delivered by a parent clutching a double Scotch. High-school principals are no longer surprised when a parent says, "Thank God he's only drunk" when they report that Junior is staggering around the school bouncing off the walls.

A recent survey of 10,000 New York City junior and senior high-school students showed that 12 percent of the students reported a pattern of drinking that can be classified as alcoholic or problematical. Eighty percent of the students surveyed drank to some exent, most of them occasionally, and in limited amounts. Many of the youths believed that the abuse of alcohol is a "less harmful" means of dealing with peer pressures, family problems, and social aggressiveness than drugs.

It would be a serious mistake to infer from these examples that the problem of student drinking exists only in schools in the larger cities. A study conducted at a suburban high school in Illinois by the Columbia School of Public Health and Administrative Medicine found that 34.1 percent of the students had used marijuana, 18.2 percent had used barbiturates, 15.7 percent used amphetamines, 26 percent used LSD or other psychedelics, while 8.2 percent had tried cocaine and 4.7 percent had experimented with heroin.

The superintendent of that school stated: "The superintendent that says he does not have a drug problem in his high school either is guilty of a shameful cover-up or he just does not know the facts."

Citizens of Anthony, New Mexico (population 1,728) would probably agree with the Columbia study's statistics. They would definitely agree that drug-related violence is manifest in the schools. Two plainclothes police officers were on the Anthony High School campus talking to a student suspected of dealing drugs. Angry students stoned the policemen, damaged their vehicles, and raised so much hell it took tear gas to break up the riot, which ended with sixty students being arrested.

A 1974 report, "Crime in the Schools," issued by the Select Committee on Crime of the New York State Legislature, revealed that there were student-run brokerages in some of New York City's high schools that offered the services of youthful male and female prostitutes! One boy I personally interviewed claimed that half the students in his Brooklyn junior high school hustled at one time or another. A former boy hustler, appearing on Tom Snyder's "Tomorrow" show on NBC, said that most of his fellow students were hitting the streets from time to time.

The street urchin, like Bart, who was mentioned earlier, very quickly learns that his new life-style is made much easier with drugs. Grass gives a nice euphoric glow that makes the body feel a newly-discovered sensual delight. The boy's adult companion is well aware of this. One of them said, "I've never started a kid out on drugs and I don't think I ever would. I don't have to. They already know about it. But I use it with them. They'd rather go for a lid of grass than fifteen bucks. After we've smoked a couple of numbers together, any inhibitions he might have just float away with the smoke." But in this respect, very few of the hustlers are taken advantage of. To them, the exchange of body for grass has a profit motive. One kid said he can start his evening with a lid of grass from his first customer and sell it to the next for a higher price. The boy will then pay cash to buy a lid of mediocre grass that will be sold to his next customer at a higher price. This parlay continues to a point where an evening's work can show a substantial profit.

Reports of boys being forced into prostitution by pimps through the use of drugs are rare, but not unknown. One chicken hawk in New York recalled that on several occasions a pimp delivered to his apartment boys who were high on heroin. "I stopped doing business with him," he said. "In the first place, they're no good sexually if they're stoned on smack and besides one of the boys told me he didn't want to do anything . . . that the pimp kept him stoned to sell him."

Another New Yorker told *Newsweek*'s Jerome Gram, "I remember one pimp calling me to say he had a nice thirteen-year-old he had just broken in. I went over and found the most beautiful kid I've ever seen. But here was this child, handcuffed to a bed, crying desperately. The pimp had raped the boy and then burned his initials into his buttocks with a cigarette. I gave the pimp fifty dollars and took the boy to a hospital."

In Los Angeles, an adult spent days looking for his sixteen-year-old friend who had mysteriously disappeared. Acting on a tip, the man tracked the boy to a sleazy hotel room. The boy, semi-conscious on heroin, was lying face down on a grubby bed. His "provider" had four men waiting in the hallway to use the boy at ten dollars apiece. The boy had already been serviced by four others and, based on later information from a doctor, it was one of the first four that had gonorrhea.

# 13

# Sex Education and the Bible

*"I don't want my son
to be a sissy. . . ."*

Sex education is one of the most controversial subjects in school systems throughout the country—a subject that strikes fear in the hearts of most school administrators. It is pointless to list those schools that teach anything approaching sex education and those that don't. Suffice it to say that most schools avoid the issue completely—usually after being pressured by "concerned parents" whose opposition is based on the reverse theory that what students know might hurt them. Despite the skyrocketing rate of teen-age pregnancies and venereal disease, those schools that do have some form of instruction usually pussyfoot around and manage to turn a fascinatingly complex subject into an exercise in boredom. In most cases, schools, guided by parents, decide what their students should know about sex. Almost always, the end result is a watereddown lecture on basic biology.

Some states have authorized classes in which children learn about the causes, effects, and prevention of venereal diseases and the functions of their reproductive organs. But that's about as far as the states are prepared to go. They're certainly not about to let schools teach such loaded subjects as birth control and morality, premarital sex and abortion. Before students are even allowed to take the instruction that is permitted, parents are required to be notified in advance in some states so they might have the opportunity to study the course material to make sure they find it suitable. They are also provided with a form to sign if they don't want their children to attend the class. There are indications that some of the parents should consider taking the course themselves rather than forbidding their children to attend. There was even a case in California where the sex-education teachers themselves were denied instruction. A bill was recently introduced in the California Legislature to establish family-life in-service training to prepare teachers. It passed both houses and was promptly vetoed by then governor Ronald Reagan.

From the parents' point of view, the safest way to deal with their child's new sexual awareness is to ignore it and hope the children will handle it on their own—as they themselves did when they were children. But today's children face a far greater challenge. Their newly-discovered sexual potential is fueled by a new wave of moral sanctions that encourage sexual activity, so they turn elsewhere for answers to sex questions and find them in television, movies, pornographic material, and music.

Our youngsters' preoccupation with sex is clearly heard in the lyrics of the songs sung by rock groups (today's rock stars providing the role models once found in baseball and football players). Most parents reject the music because it's "much too loud and I can't understand what they're saying anyway." If they would listen, they would find that the songs deal either with free love, the advantages (and sometimes the disadvantages) of drugs, or anti-establishment feelings. (Remember that the kids were singing about the immorality of the Vietnam War long before the adult population found it fashionable to join in.) As rock music and its message progressed, so did the presentation of sex. In the last two years, the music switched from acid-rock to glitter-rock, with Alice Cooper and David Bowie appearing in semi-drag, reaching out to be a little more outrageous than Mick Jagger and the Rolling Stones. Jay Ehler, a music critic and social observer, made these comments in the *Los Angeles Free Press*:

"There wasn't a single album the Stones created that didn't have some overt, specific sexual reference. As the albums continued, the Rolling Stones dipped deeper into their own uncharted, chaotic mythos as their style became more apparent to them. To a sexually-developing, role-forming young audience ready for the next musical thing, Jagger appealed in his almost para-sexual, god-like visage to young men and women alike. He did what he wanted to and because he was on a pedestal above the crowd, it was 'cool' for any and all to 'get off' on him. On his pedestal, Jagger offered fantasies for everyone who cared to partake—hereto, trans, bi and homo. Mick Jagger and Keith Richards thumbed their noses at the sexual mores that had existed before and wrote a few new chapters in a very old book, safely camouflaged behind the purity and innocence of music.

"The group wholeheartedly, and perhaps unwittingly, popularized three of man's most human endeavors within their style. They were a flaunt with possible evil; a brush with eventual mayhem; a squirming, slithering romp through an adolescent analysis of bodily behaviors. They rose from a dingy, salt-of-the-earth type existence, as fictitiously real as it was, from dark rooms and obfuscated corners where shadows of men juiced themselves off with the dexterities of their own hand and women made love to Coke bottles, and where male and female lusted on one another for personal pleasures.

"This was the allure of the Rolling Stones: doing everything, or virtually everything, a middle-class American youth had been raised to believe was sinful. The Stones were a first blow job, a first fuck, a first snort of cocaine, a first toke of grass. They were rear entry, mutual masturbation, lust, carnal knowledge and openly displayed behind-closed-door thrills, cheap and/or otherwise. They were a catalyst to do; new thoughts to try.

"Richards and Mick Jagger," concluded Ehler, "were apostles, not of Christ, but of Lucifer."

With the majority of parents clinging to "the-stork-brought-you" explanation, one can readily imagine what happens when schools attempt to bring in speakers who talk about homosexuality. In nearly all cases, the end result is a march on the school by angry parents, horrified at the thought that their children should even be exposed to the fact that homosexuality exists. They would much prefer to stay with the "man in the dirty raincoat" myth and let it go at that.

A high-school course that included lectures on homosexuality was recently the subject of a tremendous uproar in Santa Barbara, California. It all started when the high-school paper announced that the course included information on abortion, premarital sex, contraception, and homosexuality. Parents immediately banded together under the official title of "Concerned Parents" and claimed the "family life" course was advocating immorality. Spokesmen for the group denounced the course as promoting "sewer standards" and as "the final blow of a degenerate community."

Dr. Harry Haldeman told the school board: "When you pervert or distort the system, you will bring perversity into the home. If you believe that people can't be led into homosexuality, you are wrong. It is possible to take a normal child and pervert him. Only about ten percent of homosexuals ever recover and they have no right to come into our schools and influence our children."

Dr. Haldeman, presumably unwittingly, had neatly restated one theory that grips much of the country: homophobia. The theory is that if you are exposed to a homosexual, you become one. If you listen to what a homosexual teaches, you become a homosexual. The statement "Only about ten percent of homosexuals ever recover . . ." indicates that Dr. Haldeman equates homosexuality with leukemia or subscribes to the recently (and officially) debunked myth that homosexuals are mentally sick.

In the Santa Barbara case, the "Concerned Parents" lost. Dr. Evelyn Hooker, a research psychologist known and respected for her studies of male homosexuality, told the audience that conversion to homosexuality is a myth. She defended the course for ventilating topics that young people "are usually afraid to talk about."

After speeches from both sides, including an impassioned shout from one man that everyone involved would "go to hell," the board, by a four-to-one vote, decided to retain the course. Board members also took the opportunity to commend the course instructor whose methods had come under fire by the Concerned Parents. The lone dissenter on the board was the bishop of the local Mormon Church. At last report, Santa Barbara is still intact and there are no indications of widespread conversion to the homosexual way of life.

The lack of any significant sex education in the schools is certainly not the fault of the school system. The fault lies directly with the parents and with the churches. It is a confused mixture of morality versus education, morality versus politics, and morality versus common sense. Public-school officials have always been fearful of church intervention because it gives both parents and politicians the official backing of God and the Bible. Parents' groups, marching under the banner of decency, are invariably led by a man of the cloth. In some cases, the protests have been ridiculous and, in one particular case, ludicrous. It showed a need for sex education for the protestors.

In 1974, the *Advocate* reported that two Baptist ministers in New Milford, Connecticut, had threatened to sue school officials over a required sixth-grade home-economics class because, they said, the course encouraged homosexuality in their boys.

The Reverend Lynn Mays, a minister at the Faith Baptist Temple, said the course "usurped the authority of the home" and forced a child "into a situation that is foreign to his or her traditional role." The concerned minister explained his rationale this way: "By having a young boy cook or sew, wearing aprons, we're pushing a boy into homosexuality. It's contrary to what the home and the Bible has stood for. When God set up the human race, there was a division of sexes. A woman's place is in the home. That's where God put them, barring unusual circumstances."

The Reverend James Clemmons, Associate Minister at the same church said, "We'll take it to the U.S. Supreme Court if we have to. My son doesn't want the course and I don't want him to be a sissy."

The school refused to discontinue the program, saying youngsters liked the course and it was part of general education. Reverend Clemmons's son, eleven-year-old James, was exempted from the home-economics course, though, by the school board.

Said Clemmons, "I'm no psychologist, but I know it's true that ages nine to thirteen are the most important part of a child's sexual development. Everyone has homosexual tendencies and this feminine stuff being taught is bringing about the moral decay of children."

If the two Baptists were to carry out their threat to take th matter to the U.S. Supreme Court and file their brief based o the teachings of the Bible, it would open up a can of theologica. worms similar to Madalyn Murray O'Hair's suit that eliminated prayers in school.

❖     ❖     ❖

January 1, 1976, was an occasion for extra celebration for many in the State of California and considerable dismay for others. At the stroke of midnight, Assembly Bill 489 became law, and California joined a dozen other states in liberalizing its sex laws to conform to fact rather than fiction. The press dubbed it the "Consenting Adult Bill" while its opponents referred to it as the "Homosexual Bill of Rights."

AB 489 didn't have the easiest rite of passage. Church groups joined together and issued dire warnings that California was heading straight to hell on a pogo stick. Grim pictures were painted of homosexual teachers flocking to the classrooms bent on perverting everyone in sight. An attorney from Alhambra, California, made a series of TV appearances to point out that the wording of the bill permitted sexual intercourse with consenting animals and he tried to drum up support to have the bill placed on the 1976 general-election ballot. Whether the thought of lusting over a family's always-consenting cocker spaniel was too ludicrous, or whether the general public was becoming bored with all the furor is unimportant now. The attorney's attempt failed and AB 489 was signed into law. It permitted consenting adults to do whatever they had a mind to do, providing they did it in private and without infringing on the rights of others. The bill retained criminal penalties for sex acts with minors and non-consenting adults.

When California's Coalition of Christian Citizens launched its attack against AB 489, its main weapon was the Bible, which, ever since it was written, has been used as a club against anyone who didn't conform to Christian ethics. The Biblical teachings, the group maintained, were against all forms of sex outside the marriage institution, including masturbation. They failed to mention that the laws that forbade homosexual behavior originated from ancient Jewish sex codes that were later formalized by the Christian Church. In the sixth century, the Emperor Justinian condemned homosexual offenders to death by the sword, firmly believing that homosexuality was the cause of earthquakes (an observation to which Californians should give serious thought). This same code—the Justinian Code—was retained for over thirteen hundred years. During that time, homosexuals were punished by ecclesiastical courts, often by death and torture. In Paris, homosexuals were burned at the stake as late as the mid-eighteenth century; in England, it wasn't until the nineteenth century that the punishment was reduced to life imprisonment.

However, the California Coalition's biblical war failed. With the passage of time, the acquisition of technical knowledge, the eradication of superstition and fear, many biblical teachings are no longer considered valid or true.

Certainly, the Bible did speak against homosexuality. It also spoke against women who wear red dresses. It also spoke against other sins such as eating rabbit (Lev.11:6), lobster, clams, shrimp, oysters (Lev. 11:10-12), rare steak (Lev. 17:10), and wearing wool and linen at the same time (Deut. 22:11).

It is not accepted nowadays that the emission of semen renders a male unclean or that the sexual act is unclean as it is stated in Leviticus 15:16-18.

It is not acceptable nowadays that a woman is so unclean during the menstrual period that everything she touches, sits on, or lies on is also rendered unclean and must undergo ritual cleaning (Lev. 15:19-28).

It is not accepted nowadays that persons must be put to death for committing adultery (Lev. 20:10).

The problem with quoting the Bible to further one's own view of homosexuality is that the Bible does not now say precisely what it once did. It has been bent and twisted through centuries of transliteration, translation, and interpretation. It has been vulnerable to human error and to some seemingly deliberate distortions. For example, the most widely used Bible today is the King James version. In Romans 1:26-27 it says:

*For this cause God gave them up unto vile affections: for even their women did change the natural use into that which is against nature: And likewise also the men, leaving the natural use of women, burned in their lust one toward another. . . .*

The translation called "Good News for Modern Man" puts it a little differently. It says:

*Because of what men do, God has given them over to shameful passions. Even the women pervert the natural use of their sex by unnatural acts. In the same way men give up natural sexual relations with women and burn with passion for each other.*

The J. B. Phillips translation has another presentation:

*God therefore handed them over to disgraceful passions. Their women exchanged the normal practices of sexual intercourse for something which is abnormal and unnatural. Similarly the men, turning from natural intercourse with women, were swept into lustful passions for one another.*

Essentially, the two interpretations of the King James version say the same thing, but which one is closest to the original? Gerald Larue is Professor of Biblical History and Archaeology at the University of Southern California's School of Religion. In an article for the *Los Angeles Times* entitled "The Bible: Shaky Ground for Homosexual-Haters" he warns: "Those who use the Bible as a weapon should be consistent—accept all of it, or justify the selection of a few passages to the exclusion of others. Better yet, they might apply selected biblical passages to their own lives, not to the lives of others."

Larue adds: "To interpret laws and regulations with concern for the human rights of others requires moving beyond the letter of the law to the principles of individual rights and the freedom to differ. Adherents of religious groups who attempt to use the Bible as a social weapon have lost sight of these important precepts, and have been caught up in legalism that emphasizes marginal details open to varying interpretations."

In Matthew, Jesus is reported as saying that if a man looks lustfully at a woman, it is the equivalent of having sexual relations with her. Jesus is also reported to have said there could be no divorce except on the grounds of adultery, a piece of impractical foolishness prescribed to by the state of New York until quite recently. And again, Jesus is also reported to have said that anyone who marries a divorced woman commits adultery. The proponents of the Bible would do well to consider what the enforcement of these teachings would mean in today's society where one out of three marriages ends in divorce. Remember, in the days of the Bible, Israel was a very small nation, surrounded by enemies, and needed to "multiply" just in order to survive.

The scripture most often used against homosexuals is in the Old Testament, Genesis 19:1-28, which describes the destruction of Sodom and Gomorrah. According to many church groups and ministers, the twin cities were destroyed because of the sin of homosexuality. But Jeremiah and Ezekiel do not subscribe to that idea. They say:

> I have seen also in the prophets of Jerusalem an horrible thing: they commit adultery, and walk in lies: they strengthen also the hands of evildoers, that none doth return from his wickedness: they are all of them unto me as Sodom and the inhabitants thereof as Gomorrah (Jer. 23:14).
> Behold, this was the iniquity of thy sister Sodom, pride, fulness of bread, and abundance of idleness was in her and in her daughters, neither did she strengthen the hand of the poor and needy.

*And they were haughty and committed abomination be-
fore me: therefore I took them away. . . .* (Ezek. 16:49-50).

To say that Sodom and Gomorrah were destroyed for
their homosexuality is incorrect. God destroyed the cities because he couldn't find ten righteous people in Sodom (Gen.
18:32). As a punishment for their wickedness, ". . . the Lord
rained upon Sodom and upon Gomorrah brimstone and fire
from the Lord out of heaven; And he overthrew those cities, and
all the plain, and all the inhabitants of the cities, and that which
grew upon the ground." (Gen. 19:24-25). Presumably the word
"sodomy" is a derivation of the name Sodom, though why that
city got stuck with the bad reputation, and Gomorrah got away
relatively scot-free, is not clear.

But the pros and cons of the Bible and the ups and downs
of Sodom mean little or nothing to the young boy leaping head-
long into a sexually confused society. He has questions and he
wants answers. Chances are he won't get them from his parents,
his school, or his church. So he'll turn to his peers for answers
and they'll blunder along together, guessing and conjecturing,
reaching conclusions by committee, not by authority.

PART

# III

## THE
## CURE

# 14

# A Department of Education and Youth?

*"I'm sure it can be done . . . if we really want it."*

September 22, 1975, was a bad day for the Sears, Roebuck store in Dyersburg, Tennessee. The crudely-wrapped package contained a bundle of torn-out pages from the Sear's catalog. The enclosed note said that if the marked items weren't delivered, together with three new Peterbilt trucks, the store would be bombed. The total tab of the requested items reached the one-million-dollar mark and included rifles, shotguns, and ammunition as well as a substantial amount of farm equipment. The police moved quickly and traced the package (which was easy to do because it had arrived with insufficient postage). They arrested five juveniles between ages of ten and fourteen. Officers said later it was more than just a prank—if the youngsters' demands hadn't been so high, they might have gotten away with it.

Also that year, in Los Angeles, a fourteen-year-old boy was charged with murder and twenty-six other crimes. His record showed sixteen arrests by the time he was twelve. His first arrest had been when he was nine.

In Los Angeles, a Superior Court jury deliberated for four days before convicting Dan Yert, twenty-nine, on nine counts of lewd conduct and sexual acts involving two thirteen-year-old boys. One of the boys testified he had been dangled over a cliff by two policemen to get him to reveal names of other men with whom he had sex.

And in Houston, Texas, as Wayne Henley sat in his cell serving out three life sentences for his part in the murder of twenty-seven boys, one of his guards, twenty-year-old Robert Weidner, was indicted by a grand jury on two charges of committing sodomy with two prisoners.

In Rockford, Illinois, the frozen body of the fifteen-year-old son of an alderman was discovered in a cabin. The boy had disappeared twelve days previously while delivering morning newspapers. He was the third newspaperboy to disappear in three years. The first two had been abducted, spray-painted, and sexually molested before they were released.

These are not isolated cases. They are part of hundreds of similar stories that clatter out of the wire-service machines every day in newsrooms across the nation. The popular belief is that the young adult years are a boy's happiest, with the fewest cares and responsibilities in the world. Unfortunately this isn't borne out by the facts.

Two hundred youngsters, between fourteen and seventeen, per 100-thousand population are being committed to mental hospitals. Teen-age suicide has tripled in the last ten years and now runs at the rate of thirty a day. Juvenile crime has increased by 1,600 percent in twenty years. Police officials in Phoenix, Arizona, estimate that 80 percent of all illegal violations are committed by juveniles.

When you take the interlocking elements of vandalism and violence in the schools, failure of the school system itself, fractured families and broken homes, failure of the juvenile justice system, disrespect for law and order, and the standing army of disenfranchised and disenchanted youth, the need for sweeping reform is glaringly obvious. The one million runaways wandering around the country are not only symbols of rebellious youth; they are also symbols of our failure as adults to inspire and direct. Until we are adult enough to face that uncomfortable fact, there is very little hope for a solution. Indeed, the question today seems to be whether a solution even exists.

Taken collectively the thousands of agencies, foster homes, juvenile police officers, detention centers, crash pads and halfway houses, judges and social workers—all the elements in the booming kid business—are a palpitating mass of indecision.

State standards collide with federal standards and the disparities between the states themselves have to be seen to be believed. As we have seen, the public-school system is a series of convulsing bureaucracies more preoccupied with law and order than with anything remotely approaching education. Parents are bewildered and have no idea where to turn when confronted with the problem child. Juvenile experts bemoan the skyrocketing rate of juvenile delinquency. *Newsweek's* September 8, 1975, issue quoted Joseph B. Williams, Chief Justice of New York City's Family Court as saying, "There are no quick answers. All of a sudden, the juvenile justice system is supposed to come up with an answer that wipes out all the experiences in a child's life and all that has been done to him. I don't think any system can do that."

Perhaps not; certainly not the system we have now.

With all the statistics of failure it seems apparent that the system has to be changed. Not modified; not adjusted. Changed from top to bottom, starting at square one. It will take time, money, and commitment, but it can be done. To do it properly will require major surgery that should start in Washington.

Why not take Education away from the Department of

Health, Education, and Welfare and establish a new Cabinet-level department called the Department of Education and Youth. Place a Ralph Nader, consumer-advocate type of person at the helm instead of a politician (or a politician who is a Ralph Nader type). DEY would be charged with the overall responsibility for everything related to youth development, including education to the college level, reconstruction of the juvenile justice system, reconstruction of the public-school system, and preparation of youths for their eventual entry into the labor market. And—most important—make DEY openly accountable to the public.

Let DEY set basic educational standards that require a person to read, write, and handle basic math before he or she is graduated from high school. Restructure the school curricula so that the college-bound student can proceed quickly and smoothly toward his academic goals. Make similar provisions for students who are not college-oriented, who have a different mission, but who must be prepared for fitting-in, not dropping-out.

Let DEY, working closely with labor leaders, create vocational training schools within the public-school system. Set up the schools as mini-factories that produce products for sale. Train the boys who attend these schools for worthwhile jobs in the fashion of the Junior Achievement program. There are plenty of products, no longer being manufactured in the United States but imported as components for American-made products, that can be made and sold. The program might produce some anguished cries from other countries now selling us these goods, but the money saved from fighting juvenile crime would probably offset that lost by importing cheaper foreign products. Besides, isn't the cost of our children's lives more important than lower prices?

Let DEY re-examine the so-called voucher system as an alternative to the public-school system, not as a replacement for it. The voucher system is one in which parents could elect to receive a monetary grant from the federal government each year to send their children to private schools. Proponents of the voucher system claim its adoption would create thousands of small, private, neighborhood schools and give parents a choice as to what type of school they want their children to attend. Parents could choose a parochial school, a school dedicated to stern discipline, a school strong on athletics, or a remedial school, to name just a few. Proponents argue that this kind of school would attract better teachers, since schools, to compete for parents' money, would be forced to provide outstanding teachers who, in turn, would have to produce good students.

Predictably, the strongest opposition to the voucher system comes from people within the public-school system. While most opponents agree that small private schools would be able to offer reduced class size and thus more individual attention, they warn of other social dangers. They argue that giving parents their choice of schools would shatter the concept of integration. They point out that small private schools for blacks would open in black communities while white areas would have exclusively white schools. The argument is, in effect, that private schools would prohibit enforced school integration.

But that argument is only valid if the voucher system completely replaces the public-school system. It is not valid if the voucher system is offered as an alternative, since federal law would still require the integration of public schools. Even James Coleman, the principal author of the government-sponsored Coleman Report of 1966 (which started the integration program rolling) admits now that the idea of bussing is self-defeating. Coleman says he still feels integrated classes are desirable but are only feasible "with the active cooperation of the middle-class families." He adds that his proposed integration plan failed because of the white flight to the suburbs and because of the fear of disorder in the schools.

If Coleman has the courage to admit his idea failed, we should at least have the courage to agree with him. The main issue in any school system is education. But it's doubtful whether any student, black or white, gets much in the way of education when riding to school in a bus guarded by armed men and then having to face the rest of the day worrying whether there will be violence in the school itself.

To continue with the Department of Education and Youth, let DEY set up and operate three federally-funded training schools for juvenile officers, juvenile judges, and juvenile social workers respectively. These schools should provide for at least two years of intensive training in youth-related subjects, with provision for periodic refresher classes on a local level, taught by a touring team of instructors. These teachers could also serve in a dual capacity as inspectors and evaluators.

The basic requirement for all candidates to any DEY program must be an appreciation of, and an enthusiasm for, working with kids and their problems. Unless that requirement were met, everything else would be pointless. Juvenile officers should be highly-specialized men dedicated to the idea that their main function is to keep kids *out* of the juvenile-justice system, not get them into it; to work *with* kids, not against them. Properly handled, the job would eventually become the most sought-after in police work. As things stand now, too many police departments staff their juvenile divisions with incompetents and misfits. In some cases juvenile officers have been assigned to the field as punishment and sent out to bash the heads of those they see as their enemies. DEY officers should be plainclothes units working in unmarked cars. They should be dedicated to developing a rapport with the kids in their assigned districts. It would take time to overcome the antagonism that currently exists between kids and police, but the latter must come to realize that recognition and respect of police authority are two different things: the one is granted; the other has to be earned.

Most police officers are enthusiastic about these ideas. Captain Clyde Cronkhite is the Commander of the Los Angeles Police Department Juvenile Division. He agrees with the basic idea, suggests some modifications, and has some innovative ideas of his own.

"I don't think there's any doubt that both money and manpower have to be directed into the juvenile level and it's going to take a lot of both," he exclaimed. "But I think it's going to take more than that. There's going to have to be major changes in juvenile law to differentiate between the so-called status offenders and the hard-core juvenile criminals."

"As things stand now," he said, "there are a lot of juvenile offenders on the streets who should be locked up; boys with records a mile long who are turned loose by the courts either because the courts don't know what to do with them or because they know what to do and are reluctant to do it."

Cronkhite pointed out that a number of men in his department, and others in the fire department, work as "big brothers" to a number of delinquents and pre-delinquents. They despair, however, over the negative effect of boys' peers. "How can you teach a boy responsibility and the difference between right and wrong, when all around him are other boys who make weekly trips to juvenile court and are sent right back on the street without any kind of punishment. The borderline kid sees every day that crime does indeed pay and acts accordingly."

Cronkhite believes that while a national academy for juvenile officers would be a good idea, the necessity of a two-year program might be doubtful. "I think a year would be sufficient providing there were provisions for additional training at the local level to encourage juvenile workers to finish their college degrees."

But Cronkhite warned, "The program won't work unless there's a massive educational thrust at all levels of juvenile work, particularly in the juvenile courts. Prior to the Gault decision (to be discussed shortly) the juvenile courts were run

informally with the idea of the best interests of the child over-
riding all other considerations. Since the Gault decision was
handed down, the courts have become like adult courts, with
defending attorneys taking an adversary position that is often
not in the best interest of the child at all."

Cronkhite's observations about juvenile courts are valid.
They are presided over by a mishmash of political appointees
who face overcrowded calendars, hostile parents, bewildered
children, and poorly-prepared cases. All too often the fate of a
child is not determined by the merits of the case but by the
availability of facilities. Young thugs are turned back onto the
streets daily because juvenile detention centers are already
overflowing.

In most cities, juvenile courts are centrally located, creating problems for parents who have to take the day off from
work to appear. Probation departments are often located elsewhere, as are the holding facilities. One solution to this problem
seems obvious: neighborhood courts. Let DEY, working with
local and state officials, set up neighborhood facilities—thousands of them if necessary—planned and designed to serve the
community. It's not necessary, or even desirable, to build new
buildings. Rather, buy older four- or five-bedroom houses and
convert them. In larger communities it might be desirable to
buy an entire block of old homes in order to create a juvenile
complex consisting of a court, juvenile officers' and social workers' facilities, short-term holding facilities, and temporary shelters where a young person could go to "cool off" after disputes
with his parents.

Hire, don't appoint, juvenile directors or commissioners
(get rid of the term "judge") who needn't have law degrees.
After two years at the suggested national academy they should
be well versed in juvenile law. Provision could be made for
federal grants to those who wish to extend their legal knowledge. Forget such foolishness as age, height, and weight re-

quirements. Select these very important men for their common sense. There's a wealth of available talent among senior citizens —spry, active men and women who think young and would enjoy the work rather than be horrified by it. By the same token, there is a wealth of talent among the young—people who have been operating crash pads, foster homes, and crisis centers.

The court's staff should include an adequate number of practicing attorneys, clerks, social workers, and counselors. These people would work directly with the families of juveniles and act as liaisons with the schools. Some staff members should even teach in the schools. There should be a qualified person to teach sex education either on a family basis or on a one-to-one basis.

However, in order for any reorganization of our juvenile facilities to be successful, another more important change must take place: the reorganization of juvenile law, clear definition of what constitutes juvenile delinquency, and agreement on just what rights a child has under the law.

# 15

# Juvenile Justice?

*"Such a son
shall be put to death."*

There is currently before the Senate Judiciary Subcommittee on Criminal Laws and Procedures the Criminal Justice Reform Act of 1975 (S-1), which will attempt to revise and codify federal criminal law. The fact that it took nine years to write the act's 753 pages is a graphic indication not only of the need for the change, but of the disarray of the laws of the land. The record of committee testimony alone runs well over eight thousand pages. Even if the act passes, experts say it might take another ten or fifteen years for federal judges to work out the exact meaning of all its provisions. S-1 has already aroused bitter controversy and, with the expected flood of amendments (Senator Bayh plans to offer fifteen), it might be a long time before it ever does become law. Whether it passes or not, the stakes are high because every citizen will have to live with the results for decades to come.

Although the juvenile-justice system has made considerable progress over the years, laws pertaining to juveniles have not kept pace with society's ever-changing moral stance. England's fifteenth-century laws gave local communities the power to "regulate and control the young, poor, and criminal," with the provision that children between five and fourteen years of age were to be prepared by local officials for agricultural services. In 1563, England started its system of apprenticing young boys of ten to craftsmen. In essence this method is still used in England today.

The theory behind apprenticeship was that local authorities could sell an impoverished child to a craftsman as a "trainee" or "assistant," so that he might learn a trade and thereby fit smoothly into society. For all practical purposes it was a device to get cheap labor. The boy, in return for his services, was provided with room, board, and little else until he learned his craft and grew old enough to fend for himself—or until he ran away. (There was recently a modern-day version of apprenticeship. Fourteen-year-old Juan Guzman ran away from a New Jersey home for delinquents. He approached a farmer on the street and asked if he could do some chores for the man in exchange for a place to live. The farmer went with the boy to see the woman with whom Juan had been staying and "after some haggling" gave her three chickens in exchange for the boy's services. Maria Guzman said, "If my son is happy where he is, I would rather have him happy with the people on the farm than unhappy with us in Newark.")

The indenture system was one idea brought to the United States from England. In New England, dependent children were apprenticed while poor children and adults were auctioned off either individually or as family units to owners of almshouses. In 1646, a Massachusetts Bay Colony statute decreed that if a man had "a stubborn or rebellious son" of at least sixteen years of age, he could bring him to the magistrate's court where "such a son shall be put to death." These abominable conditions prevailed for more than two hundred years. Children were treated as chattels rather than as persons. At the turn of the twentieth century, the first changes came about when reformers, lobbying for women's rights, also discovered the plight of the children.

In 1899, Illinois became the first state to pass a juvenile act. California passed its Juvenile Court Act in 1903 and, by 1925, forty-six states had created special courts and judicial procedures for children. The first known study of juvenile facilities came in 1920, in California. Some of the comments made in that report bear a startling resemblance to comments being made today:

"A. There is a lack of agreement among the counties as to the proper function of a detention home. There is no established policy on the following essential matters:

1. *As to the type of persons being detained.*
In some instances, adults including the sick and blind, have been cared for with the children. In a few counties, dependent as well as delinquent children are placed in detention homes.

2. *As to the purpose of detention.*
In some of the nine counties, the detention homes are used for correctional purposes and children are committed for a definite period. In a number of other counties, the home is used for dependent children and resembles an orphanage rather than a detention home. In others, it is used as a place for temporary detention of delinquent minors pending examination and final disposition of the courts.

"B. There is a lack of necessary equipment for medical examination and scientific research.

"C. There is no uniformity regarding location of detention homes and their relation to court and probation offices.

1. Detention homes in some counties are located on county hospital grounds. This proximity with the county indigent is undesirable.

2. Detention homes in some of the counties are long distances from the court and probation offices and are not easily accessible.

"D. There is no accepted form of detention-home records, therefore, an effort should be made to standardize detention-
home administration along these lines."

It is clear from this Report of Agents for Juvenile Courts,
made by the State of California Board of Charities and Corrections, that while the intervening years have seen literally thousands of "studies" done on the juvenile problem, very little has
been done to correct the problems themselves. Indeed, it wasn't
until 1967, when a landmark ruling was handed down by the
U.S. Supreme Court, that an immediate effect on juvenile justice was felt—and a boy in Arizona became one of the historic
figures in American jurisprudence.

Gerald Gault may have thought it was just a joke when he
made a phone call to a woman neighbor in Globe, Arizona, and
". . . made remarks or questions of the irritatingly offensive,
adolescent variety." If Gault had been an adult, the offense,
classified as a misdemeanor, would have carried a maximum
sentence of sixty days. But Gault was only fifteen years old. At
the court hearing, Gault appeared without an attorney, the of-
fended neighbor never publicly testified, no hearing transcript
was kept, and no appeal was possible. It took a writ of habeas
corpus and two long years to get the case before the U.S. Supreme Court and to get Gault out of jail. He had been sentenced
to the State Industrial School until he was twenty-one . . . a six-
year term. The court ruled, in 1967, that when juveniles face the
threat of a jail sentence, they are entitled to be represented by
an attorney, to notice of the charges against them, and to the
privilege against self-incrimination. The Court declared that
". . . neither the Fourteenth Amendment nor the Bill of Rights
is for adults alone."

The landmark ruling gave the juvenile offender many
rights that adults had taken for granted but that had been lack-

ing for the young offender. Even so, it hardly signaled full legal rights for juveniles. The status of children in the courts is still being tested by child-advocate and legal groups hoping to get full legal rights for the young; the same rights accorded adults. The Children's Defense Fund, in Washington, D.C., is challenging the authority of a parent to commit a child to a mental institution indefinitely without a hearing; while in Atlanta, Georgia, the American Civil Liberties Union wants a state court to rule that status offenders (those charged with minor offenses) be confined in community centers, not in penal institutions.

A Department of Education and Youth could, and should, coordinate these efforts in order to resolve the obvious inequities in juvenile law and children's rights. Until these important issues are resolved, everything else is rather pointless.

In late 1974, U.S. District Judge William W. Justice handed down what could become the most important juvenile decision since Gault. Justice condemned the entire Texas reform-school system for its "widespread physical and psychological brutality" and charged that juveniles were not rehabilitated but "warehoused." In a 204-page opinion, Justice said the inmates of the school were beaten and tear-gassed as punishment for bad behavior, and, without any medical supervision, given tranquilizers to quiet them. The judge ordered Texas to close two of its reform schools and convert the rest to halfway houses and group homes. Officials of the Texas Youth Council announced they would appeal the decision because of the costs involved in making such a change. What makes the Justice opinion so important is that the U.S. Supreme Court will eventually be asked to render judgment on the conditions applicable to juvenile incarceration. That decision would apply to, and affect, every state in the Union.

The two Texas schools involved in the Justice opinion were

the Gatesville State School for Boys and nearby Mountain View, the maximum-security facility. To a passer-by, the Gatesville School looked like a well-endowed junior-college campus. The modern, low-lying brick buildings were neatly laid out with not a confining wall, steel bar, or chain-link fence in sight. The guards, smartly dressed in khaki uniforms with natty brown trim, wandered around unarmed, keeping an eye on their young wards as they moved with military precision from schoolroom to dormitory to manicured playing fields.

Visitors to Gatesville—especially state legislators with control over state funds—were met by congenial supervisors and escorted through the facility, occasionally pausing to ruffle the hair of some little tow-headed kid in a friendly manner. There were the ten-year-olds, deeply engrossed in a math class. Over here, the fourteen-year-olds, listening intently to an instructor demonstrating the art of bricklaying. There were shouts from the ball fields where the boys were playing baseball. When the visitors left, the shouts continued.

But there were unheard shouts from the lockup as kids were beaten by the guards; there were shouts as the tear gas rolled into a cell and burned open wounds like a red-hot iron; there were shouts from whippings with TV antenna wire; shouts from a drunken guard as he smashed his way into a dorm, wrecked the inmates' Christmas tree, and stomped several kids; shouts from the baseball field as a two-guard team slowly and deliberately crushed the testicles of a fourteen-year-old boy serving time for truancy.

These are all documented cases exposed by a television news team from Corpus Christi, Texas, in a documentary called "Trouble in the Reformatory." The film triggered a wave of public indignation and provided a two-week field day for the Texas press. It also forced the Texas State Senate to conduct an "investigation" that turned into a mini-Watergate. As one state official helplessly put it, "Political snowballs don't roll all the way down the hill in Texas. They get part way ... stop ... and quickly melt." But this snowball didn't melt. It sat for several years and then started to trundle downhill again, pushed by two attorneys and an investigative reporter from El Paso, Texas. Attorneys Steve Bercu and Peter Sandman filed suit against the Texas Youth Council on behalf of Alicia Morales *et al*, while reporter Bill Payne was busily exposing corruption in the El Paso County juvenile facilities. It was the Morales case that brought the ruling from Judge William Justice.

In the course of his investigation, Bercu found that homosexual activity was rampant in the two schools. "Homosexuality runs at a very high rate, approximately ninety percent in the girls' school and at a slightly lower rate in the boys' school." This is a continuing problem not only in Texas schools but in every juvenile detention home in the country. Indeed, it is safe to say that every boy incarcerated in an institution is guaranteed to be exposed to, or involved in, homosexual activity with or without his consent. One of three things will happen in a reform school: he will be forced into a homosexual act, he will force others into a homosexual act, or he'll become a willing participant and play whatever role suits his particular purpose at a particular time. The chances of him not becoming involved in homosexuality at all are rare. In Texas, the problem of controlling the sexual acts of the 1,500 boys at Gatesville and Mountain View was compounded by improper supervision by untrained personnel who seemed to define homosexuality as something that blacks did to whites, or that the strong did to the weak. Some excerpts from oral depositions taken in the Morales case show just how ludicrous the situation was at Gatesville. The questions are being asked by various attorneys for the plaintiff:

*Responding: Clarence R. Stephens, Caseworker Supervisor.*

Q. Would you explain what a Master's in Correctional Science entails?

A. Well, of course, there is about three different ones that they are . . . down at Sam Houston, Contemporary Correction and one in Police Administration and . . . I can't tell you . . . they have minors in Criminology and actually they changed that title last year or a year and a half. Of course, I started out my major and it was called Institutional Corrections with a minor in Appropriation and Parole. It is just a variety of thirty hours that you take. Of course, as you know, in the field of correction and law and society, and, you know, maybe psychology, a behavior course. I had thirty hours of it.

Q. Do any of these courses include juvenile correction?

A. I didn't have anything specifically in juvenile correction and in reading courses, reading and juvenile. Reading courses only. There wasn't any text on it. Of course, this behavior, psychopathy was the particular course on that, and then law and criminal correction, a little of that, and mostly reading courses, you know. Your intern work and the juvenile.

Q. Do any of the courses include counseling?

A. I didn't have any counseling techniques in the program.

Q. You say you are still working on your Master's thesis?

A. Well, I'm attempting to get a thesis, right. I have the thirty hours.

Q. What is the maximum number of hours that you need for your Master's?

A. Thirty hours and my thesis.

*Responding: William Wimberly, Correctional Officer 3 (Supervisor)*

Q. Before you became employed with the Texas Youth Council, what job did you have?

A. I was farming.

Q. I see. What is your education?

A. Well, I went through the eighth grade in school and then I got a G-E-D [General Educational Diploma] . . . a G-E-D a few years ago.

Q. All right. Could you tell me exactly what year it was that you got your G-E-D?

A. '62. In 1962 before we opened this school [Gatesville], while I was still working there.

Q. I forgot to ask. What is your age, sir?

A. Sixty-three.


*Responding: James Freeman, Correctional Officer 3 (Supervisor)*

Q. How long have you worked for the Texas Youth Council?

A. Sixteen years and one month.

Q. Have you always been a CO-3? [Correctional Officer 3]

A. No, sir.

Q. What other positions have you held?

A. Well, I first started over yonder on the Gatesville State School as a dorm man or dorm attendant and dog man* over there for about a year and the Mountain View School opened up and then I came over here. Then it was Supervisor, but they just changed it here lately to CO-3.

Q. So when you came to Mountain View when it opened up . . .

A. I was a supervisor.

Q. . . . it was equivalent to CO-3?

A. But it was indicated as Supervisor then.

Q. What years were you dog man at Gatesville?

A. Let's see: '61 and part of '62.

Q. I see. Before you started work for the Texas Youth Council, how were you employed?

---

* Gatesville State School maintained a kennel of mongrel dogs trained to chase any boy who tried to run away. The dogs would be followed by guards on horseback. When the boy was tracked down, he would be lassoed by the guard and dragged back to the school, sometimes face down through the unfriendly Texas cactus.

A. Well, went to the army in '55 and got out in '57 and then I started work there, but before that I was self-employed. Mostly carpenter work, and then I sheared sheep and goats, too.

Q. What is your education?

A. Well, I've got an equivalent to a high school. I took a G-E-D test.

So much for the required standards for supervisory personnel hired by the Texas Youth Council to provide control, care, guidance, and rehabilitation to 1,500 kids. TYC's conception of how the problem of homosexuality should be handled is even more ridiculous—if that's possible. All detention homes face the same problem. And there is no reason to believe that Texas has more homosexual juveniles than any other state. There is, however, plenty to indicate that the Texas juvenile-justice system helped produce many more gay kids than it had to start with. The most unenlightened of schools knew enough to separate homosexuals from the straight population. The more enlightened went one step further and separated the active homosexuals from the passive. The most enlightened provided counseling and attempted not to have a boy labeled throughout the school population.

Texas went several giant steps in the opposite direction. They segregated homosexuals into three groups: blacks in one; Anglos and Mexican-Americans in another. Then there was the third group, referred to as the "weak kids." Testimony from the Morales' depositions gave a clue to the rationale behind this rather bizarre arrangement:

*Responding: Clarence R. Stephens, Caseworker Supervisor:*

Q. How are the students assigned to the different dorms?

A. Well, the kids come in and if their social history indicates they have been involved in a passive role, you know, in homosexual activity, sometimes . . .

Q. What do you mean by passive role?

A. Say, sodomy, or if the boy has been used by another boy; the one that receives the penis of the other is the only way I can say it. That's what I call the passive role. At any rate, initially when we get a boy . . . whoever brings the folders over will set down with the Correctional Officers and they will say whether or not if a boy has been involved in any homosexual activity and the custodial staff place the boys in the dorms.

Q. The custodial staff then makes the determination as to which dorm the students go to?

A. Yes, sir.

Q. Now, you are talking about homosexuals . . .

A. Well, all of them in there are not homosexuals.

Q. Yes. You were talking about the passive homosexual. Where is the passive homosexual assigned; to what dorm?

A. Well, we have a Dorm One and a Dorm Nine where a boy of that character is placed. And like I say, it may be a kid that is not aggressive and won't take up for himself, or what have you, that you place in another dorm. You may have put him there with other boys who are not as aggressive but it will happen. We had a kid . . . come in three or four weeks ago . . . that was placed in the dorm and talk[ed] about all the boys making it hard on him. He would use the expression "make a punk out of him." They were threatening him and all, and it was recognized. He was removed from that dorm and placed in [Dorm] Nine. I asked some of the boys in there how he was doing and they say great. Everybody likes him well, where he was having a difficult time in another.

Q. How do you determine what boy goes to Dorm One and what boy goes to Dorm Nine?

A. Dorm One and Dorm Nine, you know . . . Dorm One are Negro boys and Dorm One and Dorm Nine . . .

Q. I didn't hear you.

A. Dorm One houses Negro boys and Dorm Nine are the Anglo and Latin.

*Later, in the same deposition, Stephens was questioned about what a "weak" boy was.*

A. I think that . . . now all of them are not homosexuals. . . . As I was saying, the boys are, you know, weak.

Q. Weak?

A. Yes, weak. . . . Maybe . . . you wouldn't call it homosexual, but just that he was weak and would submit to one because he needed a pack of cigarettes and this, that, and the other. And I think there were a lot of problems when they were all in the dorms. . . .

*Responding: William Wimberly, Correctional Officer 3 (Supervisor)*

Q. . . . can you give me some idea of the breakdown; what each dorm is like, what kind of boys in each dorm?

A. Well, of course, we've got them integrated as much as we can and it would be a normal, average boy in the dorm. There wouldn't be any real weak boys . . . I mean in the way of weakminded in these other dorms. We set it up as much as we can. Now, we have another dorm, Dorm Eleven, that we keep some weak boys in that can't get along with the larger boys. We have them in separate dorms, but they are integrated in this dorm.

Q. I understand that. When you say integrated, you are referring to racially integrated?

A. Yes.

Q. I understand that.

A. But the two dorms, we have the two dorms that are not integrated. That's one with colored boys and one with white and Spanish.

Q. What dorms are those?

A. Dorm One and Dorm Nine.

Q. Are those also the homosexual dorms?

A. Yes, sir.

Q. Why did they decide to separate the homosexuals along racial grounds?

A. It was just too hard to keep the boys away from them in the dorms, just too many ways that they can get to them in the dorm. It is hard enough to keep them here on the campus from getting with them, but in the dorm it certainly is a job to try and protect them.

Q. I don't quite understand what you mean by that. I understand why it is necessary to separate the homosexuals from the rest, but I don't understand why it is necessary to separate the homosexuals themselves along racial grounds. Could you explain ... what policy is there?

A. The homosexuals ... separate the homosexuals you mean from the homosexuals?

Q. Separate the boys, the homosexuals, from the white homosexuals and Negro homosexuals and Mexican-American homosexuals.

A. Well, that was because ... well, they are not all homosexuals. Just some of them are little weak boys that can't get along. They wouldn't all be in Dorm One and Dorm Nine, they wouldn't all be homosexuals.

Q. Uh huh.

A. There would be some that are just little, small, weak boys that just couldn't make it with the bigger boys.

Q. I see.

A. And it is this type of boy that is pretty hard to handle and get along. . . . You just have a lot more [sic] problems keeping them separated. It is just best. . . . It is a big enough job to handle thirty of these boys with them separated. Put them together, you've just got a double problem there.

Q. Okay.

*Responding: Mack Morris. Assistant Superintendent.*

Q. . . . Now, Dorm One and Dorm Nine, the two dorms where the boys with homosexual tendencies are sent. How is a boy sent there? What does he have to do? Obviously he has to . . .

A. Well, most of it comes in with him, record-wise, that he has been into this stuff, and we play close attention to this. We had some things develop after getting the boy over here that made us change our decision and move him down.

Q. If a boy has been assigned to another dorm and you discover that he is participating in another act with another boy, would that alone be sufficient to move him to another dorm?

A. Not necessarily.

Q. Who makes that decision?

A. Well . . . after it is investigated and it does check out, some of these cases could be cases that was that way to start with and we didn't know it. Some of these kids could be force cases. One might just force sodomy on another one.

At least one of the twenty-seven boys murdered by the Dean Corll-Wayne Henley-David Brooks trio in Houston was a Gatesville graduate. Of the forty boys I interviewed, either in the school or outside the school, all agreed they had learned one thing while they were there: they learned to hate. The hatred can be summed up in this poem written by one of the boys about the guards at Gatesville . . .

### The Man

I don't know but I've been told
When you run from Gatesville you
are subject to come back without
your soul. Be it true or be it not,

they'll never beat me up and leave
me to rot. When you run, be slick, be
fast 'cause if they catch you, that's
your ass.
Hey, hey, Check out The Man,
He will do it to you if you ain't
got no stand.
Hey, hey check out The Man,
He'll kick your ass if he gets the chance.
The Man have no regrets, The Man have no
sorrows.
If he don't get you today, he'll get you
tomorrow.

Reporter Bill Payne summed it up when he said:

"What is wrong with 'juvenile justice' in El Paso County and the State of Texas is willfully and purposefully wrong from front to back and from side to side. Juvenile justice is itself a crime involving profiteering and exploitation of children as the ends and using procedures, facilities and personnel whose finest hours, only rarely achieved, consist at most of simply ignoring the unfortunate children they vow to protect and yet almost invariably destroy."

Sid Ross, editorial consultant for *Parade* magazine, has worked for over twenty-five years as an investigative reporter. During that time he has visited hundreds of jails, detention facilities, juvenile institutions, correctional schools, and training schools all over the country. He has also attended enough seminars, conferences, conventions, and workshop sessions dealing with juvenile delinquency to hold out very little hope for improvement.

Said Ross: "From . . . what I have seen of jails, specifically in terms of juveniles, I know they are just cells and bars—a sterile, degenerating, and at times, brutalizing environment for children who are more often than not incarcerated not because they have committed horrendous offenses, but because the community or state has nothing else to offer. So you find, along with kids charged with burglary, robbery, assault, and murder the dependent and neglected kids, runaways, disturbed or retarded kids, victims of sexual abuse, victims of broken homes and so on."

Ross added: "I want to stress from my experience that the operative word is "victims," because again, many of these children, including those who have committed criminal acts, are in a very real sense the victims of society's failures."

He characterized the treatment of juveniles in prison as "benign neglect" but added, "Sometimes, when you have a number of juveniles in jail at the same time, neglect can turn into a frightening nightmare of intimidation, beatings, robberies, and homosexual rape. Instead of protective custody, you have a jungle, a ferocious jungle where the stronger and more vicious prey on the younger and the weak. Sheriffs and jailers are understandably reluctant and unwilling to supply statistics or cite examples of assaults and robberies and rapes occurring in their jails. Actually," he continued, "I believe they really do not know. The victims are scared. Would-be squealers are not deterred because of some alleged code of honor, but because they are afraid of retribution from other inmates. As a sixteen-year-old boy in a southern jail whispered to me a few months ago—this boy had recently been raped by three inmates—and I quote, 'They warned me they would split my ass up to my belly button if I squealed.'"

Ross concluded, "This is the truth, and this is why a lot of the things that surface are only the iceberg tip of what goes on in jails."

Sid Ross had been invited to testify before Senator Birch Bayh's Subcommittee to Investigate Juvenile Delinquency. *Pa-*

*rade* magazine, in 1963, had published a major story written by Ross and Ed Kiester called "Children in Jail." The story was the end result of an exhaustive investigation by the magazine's staff that probed every region of the country. It was a grim tale that revealed there were thousands of children incarcerated in prisons who had no business being there. It was the type of carefully-documented story one would think might have triggered a Senate investigation and have the public demanding immediate reform. But nothing much came of the article and, ten years later, Ross found that nothing much had changed in the juvenile justice field—except for the worse.

In September, 1972, Ross and Herbert Kupferberg wrote a lengthy article for the *Washington Post* suggesting that reform schools be shut down, and pointing out that the state of Massachusetts had done just that . . . and with notable success. The credit for the sweeping reform went to Jerome Miller, a Ph.D. from Minnesota, who had become Massachusett's Commissioner of Youth Services.

Said Miller, "Reform schools are no damn good. They neither reform nor rehabilitate and the longer you lock a kid in them, the less likely he is to make it when he gets out. They don't protect society. They're useless, they're futile, they're rotten."

With that, Miller—in three years as Commissioner—abolished Massachusetts's state-wide system for youthful offenders, saying the juvenile problems in the United States wouldn't be solved until other states shut down their institutions too. Milton G. Rector, Executive Director of the National Council on Crime and Delinquency, called Miller's decision "a courageous step in the right direction."

But Miller's reforms generated a lot of heat and a lot of opposition mostly, according to Ross, from detention guards afraid of losing their jobs and legislators who favored stern methods of dealing with delinquents. There was also strong resistance from local communities against the idea of halfway houses being operated in their area. Miller was charged with "moving too fast." He, however, scoffed at this: "You almost have to force the community to do its job. . . . There'll never be real progress without turmoil. Any reforms you make will get watered down and trickle away. The training schools are the backbone of the old system and have to be abolished. They're going the way of the almshouse."

A year after Miller took charge he held a symbolic ceremony at the Shirley Industrial School to signify his drastic changeover. "On a dark and rainy winter night," Ross wrote in his story, "ten youngsters, at a signal from the DYS chief, swung sledgehammers into the walls and bars of the solitary confinement cells in which each had spent punishment time. They left the place in a shambles."

Ross concluded: "In much the same way, Jermone Miller has made a shambles of the century-old delinquency reform structure of Massachusetts. In its place he has erected something he thinks will serve better and last longer; a system in which young delinquents are treated not as hopeless criminals but as erring humans who can win back their place in society."

Jerome Miller is now Commissioner of Children and Youth for the state of Pennsylvania, one of the few states making a genuine effort to improve its juvenile system. But conditions in general haven't changed since Miller's days in Massachusetts except, perhaps, for a growing public awareness of the scope of the problem. I asked Miller if the problem facing the country—the problem of its youth—could be diagnosed. It wasn't a particularly penetrating question, but Miller had an answer:

"I guess if one were attempting to 'diagnose' the problem of kids in our society (primarily the children of the poor), it is a matter that to the degree you are poor, disenfranchised, or that your family is relatively unstable and nonexistent, to that degree you become a captive in this society. Either you are a captive of the so-called juvenile-justice system by virtue of your illegal acts, or you are a captive of the child-welfare system by virtue of your economic deprivation and consequent limited options.

"Although I am aware of major problems confronting middle-class children as well, over the long haul these kids generally have escape hatches in terms of the relative variety of choices, options, careers, and educational varying role models etc.

"The poor, however, are quickly gathered up in one or another of the state or private (governmentally funded) programs of rehabilitation or justice . . . programs which generally' neither rehabilitate nor are just.

"In what is a competitive, generally capitalist society, these children quickly become chattel in a system whereby the providers of service make all the decisions ranging from whether or not they will accept the child into their program, to the kind of diagnoses which will be placed upon the kids and will ultimately determine the kinds of treatment or mistreatment they will receive."

Miller pointed out that Ronald Laing, the British psychiatrist, had commented that diagnoses are social prescriptions that call for certain kinds of handling and are determined by the number of options presented. Says Miller, "We diagnose children to fit the programs we devise to treat them; programs which, more often than not, are designed to produce the least cost and discomfort to the provider of the service. One has a situation in which our treatment programs in both child welfare and juvenile justice exist to reassure and comfort the service-giver rather than the recipient."

*Chapter*

# 16

# Group Homes

*"Good foster parents are
hard to find."*

The boy who becomes a ward of the court
and who has not committed a crime serious enough to be sent
to an institution is often sent to a foster home. While standards
vary from state to state, most foster homes are run by well-
meaning parents, often with children of their own, who take in
an extra child or two in exchange for a monthly stipend paid
by the placing agency. By and large it's a good program. Often
it results in the child's ultimate adoption.

One of the problems with the foster-home program is that
there aren't enough of them. Good foster parents are hard to
find for a variety of reasons and many kids suffer because of the
shortage. The foster-home concept should be expanded and im-
proved upon for certain types of children. This too could be ac-
complished by a Department of Education and Youth, working
closely in conjunction with state and local officials, which could
set up a chain of foster homes in four separate categories:

1. Temporary private-home housing run by private individuals for juveniles who have been arrested and need a
place to stay until they appear in court. These houses and the
surrogate parents who supervise them would be on call twenty-

four hours a day to provide shelter and guidance to boys without parents, boys with parents not interested in their child's problems, or boys whose problems stem from trouble in their own homes. The function of the temporary parents would be to provide transportation to and from school (if the boy is in school and no other transportation is available); to make sure the boy appears in court at the appointed time; to answer the many questions he will surely have about his future; and to reassure him that the system is working for him, not against him.

The temporary guardians would be paid on a per-boy basis plus expenses, or, perhaps, on a fixed monthly figure regardless of the number of boys housed during the month. The guardians, in addition to "normal" parents could be drawn from youth workers, police officers, ministers, or anyone else with some experience and interest in kids. Restrictions on the boys' movements would be determined by the temporary guardian. Such a program is already underway in Salt Lake City with demonstrable success. It eliminates the need for detention in a juvenile hall and all its connected problems.

2. A series of boarding houses for children who have had their cases adjudicated and who have been found to be in need of a controlled environment and professional guidance. Primarily, these homes would house status offenders with only minor emotional problems, but the house parents would have an entire battery of professionals to call upon for help. The houses would be permanent, limited to a maximum of six children, the size of a large family. The "parents" would be selected from couples whose children have already grown and are out on their own, retired couples without children, young couples without children, or para-professionals. The shelter would be run just as any other normal family organization.

It is vitally important that the housing not be labeled a "home." There is a regrettable tendency for children's shelters to hang up a shingle proclaiming it to be a "Halfway House," or a "Boy's Harbor," or whatever. This is counter-productive since it automatically stamps a kid as a waif or stray and gives the place the feel of a mini-orphanage or an almshouse. The street address is quite sufficient; there is no need to advertise its occupants as wards of the state.

3. A series of special boardinghouses, similar to those just described, but geared for children with emotional problems requiring full-time professional help. These houses would be staffed by highly-skilled social workers specializing in specific problem areas. The program would be geared to stabilize the child to a point where he could be transferred to a standard boarding home. Both private home and boardinghouse could also be used as halfway centers for the hard-core types being discharged from detention homes and on their way back into society—providing a careful evaluation of the individual showed his presence would not be in any way detrimental to the progress of permanent members of the home.

The question of placement for the young homosexual offender is difficult to resolve because of the many variables involved, mostly relating to the degree of his homosexuality.

The young, overt homosexual doesn't present too much of a problem *if* (and I emphasize if) his sexual preferences are firmly established, and if he is not a bisexual boy whose preferences are still flexible enough to enable him to choose either life-style. In the former case, the overt homosexual should be placed in a boarding home staffed by professionals, either homosexual or heterosexual, whose prime function is to help the boy develop into a productive citizen, capable of facing the problems of everyday living regardless of his sexual orientation.

The function of any controlled environment should be toward preparing a boy for the best possible life—taking into consideration his potential and his predilections—not converting him into someone he doesn't want to be, or can't be . . . and that applies equally to homosexual and heterosexual boys.

From a humanistic point of view, the young homosexual has every right to a full and productive life. For some reason, the public has never been able to accept the fact that there are young homosexuals. Society's ostrich-like approach is to consider homosexuality a condition that exists only in people over eighteen. This, of course, is nonsense. In a number of cities, parents of gay children have formed organizations to try to resolve their problems. In Hollywood, gays who are too young to drive are dropped off at gay dances by their parents. Two twelve-year-olds, arrested in a chicken-ring roundup, startled police officers by announcing they were in love with each other.

As juvenile authorities, albeit reluctantly, face the fact that there are young homosexuals and that they get into non-sexual trouble just as heterosexuals, these officials also face the problem of what to do with the kids.

Even though there are psychiatrists who claim success in "treating" homosexuals (that is, changing their orientation), there is very little evidence to support the claims. Another popular myth—that if a young homosexual is placed in a heterosexual environment he will eventually accept the heterosexual way of life—just isn't true. One only has to consider the reverse situation to depreciate the claim. Would a young heterosexual, placed in an exclusively homosexual environment, eventually become a homosexual? If the answer is "yes," it suggests that the boy in question wasn't a confirmed heterosexual in the first place. If the answer is "no," then the homosexual-into-a-heterosexual conversion doesn't hold true either. The damaging effect of placing a homosexual boy in a heterosexual environment is just as great as placing a heterosexual boy in a homosexual environment.

Authorities in Los Angeles are wrestling with this problem. An ad hoc committee was set up to produce guidelines for the county on which to base its policy, its current guidelines being woefully inadequate. After two meetings nothing was resolved except an agreement to hold further meetings. It was discovered that there were all kinds of "dangers" in reaching specific conclusions. After every proposal was met with a counter-proposal, it was decided that the "middle ground" (no motion whatsoever) was the best course of action.

The Los Angeles County counsel pointed out that the county could find itself in a difficult position if it approved the placement of young gays with gay foster parents. He suggested that, when a boy reached his eighteenth birthday, he could turn around and file suit against the county, claiming he was placed in a homosexual environment in his formative years; that if he had been placed in a heterosexual environment he might have become a heterosexual; therefore, since he is now a homosexual it is the county's fault and, therefore, the county is liable. That, the attorney said, has been the county's objection all along and that, he added, would be the county's position in the future.

Early in 1974, the Youth Service Administration (YSA) in New York approved a pilot project permitting homosexuals to serve as "big brothers" to a number of thirteen- to eighteen-year-old gay youths housed in a YSA facility. The YSA was operating a number of houses for pre-delinquent children who had no parents or whose parents refused to support them. Tom Smith, Community Services Director for the National Gay Task Force, convinced the YSA that "big brothers" who were gay could offer companionship for young gay boys on an experimental basis at one of the centers; a center used solely for young gay males. Smith said the only hurdle he could see would be in getting qualified, competent gay men to volunteer their time to be big brothers. But there turned out to be a much bigger hurdle: YSA decided to submit the entire plan to their legal department. The multiplicity of legal problems alone brought the project to an indefinite halt.

Smith, together with Steve Askanazy, Chairperson of the Gay Activists Alliance Service Committee, launched an alternative project: an attempt to have the courts assign homeless gay youths to live with gay foster parents. Although this would have been legally permissible, the actual procedure was complicated. Once a court issued such an order, the minor would become the legal foster child of the gay couple. It is extremely unlikely that a politically appointed judge would be amenable to making such a decision.

In another, later attempt in a similar direction, private child-care agencies in the New York metropolitan area quietly started a program of placing homosexual teen-age boys with homosexual foster parents. The National Gay Task Force said the program was being conducted unofficially but with the knowledge of the state division of youth.

Tom Smith said he met with state officials and found them "pretty open" to officially sanctioning the program. Smith said the program was started because the homosexual group "has gotten calls from hundreds of child-care agencies who wanted to know if we could find housing for the kids," who ranged in age from twelve to seventeen. "The agencies feel it is impossible to place an openly gay kid into a traditional foster setting," he said. "They just get tossed around from institution to institution until they reach legal age."

The National Gay Task Force does not actually place gay children with prospective gay foster parents, but refers homosexual adults to the private child-care agencies. Smith emphasized that foster fathers are screened to make sure they have no ulterior motives. He said, "Homosexual men have long been denied the opportunity to become foster fathers and a lot of gay people have expressed the desire to do so."

Ronald Gold, a spokesman for the National Gay Task Force, said it hopes for official sanction from regulatory agencies that would allow gay foster parents to be licensed and to receive child-care payments. He said the current program is a stopgap measure. "They are things we are doing simply because there are no officially structured situations in which they can be done." Gold emphasized that the program is not an effort to "proselytize" others to homosexuality and reiterates that having a homosexual foster parent will not ultimately determine the teen-ager's sexual orientation as an adult.

But homosexual foster parents will face the same problem as some of their heterosexual counterparts: the problem of not inflicting their own life-style preference on the child. There are a number of people already running successful crash pads and halfway houses who, regardless of their own sexual preferences, are perfectly capable of advising kids about sexual problems. These same people, usually young, accept the homosexual alternative as valid even though they themselves are heterosexual. The reverse also holds true. There are many dedicated, skilled homosexuals who are perfectly at home with heterosexuals (unless you prefer to believe there are no homosexual teachers, doctors, police officers, scout masters, psychiatrists, psychologists, and airline pilots who work with, guide, control, and instruct us every day of our lives).

A well-run foster home could quite easily be staffed with skilled advisers capable of discussing freely both the homosexual and the heterosexual life style. And there is no valid reason why these instructors should not be drawn from both the straight and the gay communities. A director of a boy's home in Indianapolis was questioned by Senator Birch Bayh. The Reverend Luther Hicks apparently didn't see homosexuality as a major problem. Bayh asked, "Are you able to handle some of the much-discussed and written-about traits that seem to exist in the large institutions such as homosexuality, abuse and brutality, and drug abuse? I know that it is probably too early to have a real case history on that, but do you think you are on top of it when you deal with a small number of boys?"

Hicks replied, "Yes, sir. My experience is that in this atmosphere we have not had that problem and will not. . . . They [the boys] are not in that close relation all of the time, and they are not in a setting where they see all of this sexual stuff on TV. When these lads get home in the evening, they have free time and they are permitted to go into the neighborhoods and have relationships. . . . In the kind of program we run, we do not have the necessity of being worried about homosexual behavior because the guys go out. They can entertain company and girls can come in and see them, you see, and that makes a big difference.

"Add to that," Hicks continued, "we are talking about values, we are talking about morals, and we are talking about individual responsibilities—and all this adds up to a behavior pattern. Suppose we caught a guy engaging in homosexual behavior with another guy. I guarantee you one thing that would not happen is that we would not take them both and tie them spread-eagle to the bed, or punish them. We would not make an example of them or ostracize them or criticize them if this is their pattern of behavior. We would . . . deal with the whole situation by trying to find out if it was by the consent of the two . . . why they would have to go this way . . . what their desires are when it comes to interrelationships with other people, and then send for the kind of proper treatment that might help them change their behavioral pattern."

Hicks concluded, "Now, I think this is the only wholesome approach to it; I really do."

In Houston, the Reverend Jack McGinnis thinks along the same lines. He stated "Now, if I'm going to criticize the system, I should be able to propose what to put in its place, and I will. My idea is nothing new really, but it's strangely untried. A child in need of social supervision, a delinquent child who has broken the law, does not have antisocial behavior or law violation as his primary problem. He, or she, has hurt and difficulty as their primary problem ... a very deep and painful alienation from the people he treasures the most; from the values he treasures the most.

"Now, when you talk about alienation, it assumes there had to be some valuable relationship to begin with from which the young person has been alienated. We are all born into a valuable relationship with our parents, even though we can't express it or even understand it. In the first few years of our lives we treasure that experience and the feeling of intimacy it brings. The first basic difficulty encountered is the initial alienation from the parents. That's where, in my experience, one hundred percent of the difficulties stem from. And this can happen because of death, divorce, both parents staying together but facing problems and difficulties of their own—in a thousand different ways. Somewhere along the way, there's a loss of that feeling of intimacy . . . of being loved and cared for, almost totally, and eventually being able to return that love and care. The loss causes the deepest pain to the child. The alienation from that experience, and every difficulty after that, is related.

"When a child gets to the age where society can notice his antisocial behavior, perhaps because of a violation of law, what does the system concentrate on? It concentrates on the behavior and attacks it. If you don't behave, if you don't obey the laws, if you don't change your behavior, we'll lock you up. We'll take you away from your parents. The system *adds* to the alienation instead of concentrating on its removal.

"Alienation and reconciliation are terms we are using a lot today when we're working with children in trouble. We are concentrating on ways in which we can restore or reconcile the primary invaluable relationships from which these kids have been alienated. And if it isn't possible to restore the relationships, or to reconcile the kid with his parents, or whoever ... then we should be concentrating on replacing the valuable, intimate, close, affirming, loving relationships in his life some other way. If he can't get it with the people who are valuable to him, let's supply it for him. Let's do it ourselves.

"It takes time, it takes patience, and it takes a lot of love. ... I'm convinced that far too many people, especially in probation departments and courts—people who deal with kids in trouble—just don't like kids. Can't we see that the system isn't working? If it were, we'd have less delinquency, not more. You can take the statistics that show we have more delinquency because of the increase in population and throw those right in the nearest river or lake. It just isn't true. We have more delinquency because the methods we're using to combat delinquency are the wrong methods and the juvenile justice system isn't working. It just flat isn't working.

"Why can't we find groupings of people who are capable of caring deeply for other people, especially youngsters. Group them together in kinds of communities, not communes, but groups of people who share and support one another. Take five or six couples within a neighborhood or within a certain part of the city and give them the tools that will help them: financial assistance, meetings, support, encouragement, and training. Nowadays, probation departments will just shop and find anybody to put a kid with because they have so many kids that have to be put somewhere. ... I've known many here in Houston that had five or six kids simply because they were getting up to $90 a month and what they were doing to the kids to get it was a disaster. ...

"So let's develop ways to train people. Let's develop ways of finding people who do care, who are able to do what I've been talking about all along, who are doing it already with their own children and with foster children. It's an important point to make foster care permanent. ... When the kid joins a grouping of people, or an individual, or a couple, he should know, and the foster parents should also know, that they're going to be together until that kid grows up and is able to live on his own. He may still have real parents who may visit, but it's the foster parent who is going to lay down his life for the kid. The foster parent has to be able to say, 'Look, I want you here until you grow up. I want to take care of you no matter what happens and if you get into trouble again I want to fight it with you. We'll work it out and fight it out, but we'll make it until you grow up. And I'll keep caring for you, no matter what happens until you can make it on your own.

"It can be done," insists McGinness, "and if we don't do it . . . who will?"

*Chapter*

# 17

# The Enigma
# of Boy Prostitution

*"Go to hell, man. I like
peddling my ass."*

The enigma of boy prostitution does not lend itself to a simple solution. It infuriates the police, confounds the psychiatrists, bewilders the legislators, enrages the parents and is a matter of grave concern to gay-community leaders because it perpetuates the myth that all homosexuals prey on young boys.

There are two elements in the homosexual community that unofficially embarrass the majority of gays: the very effeminate and the very young. The very effeminate male is embarrassing because, to the general public, he is representative of all gays. He is visible proof of the stereotyped image gays are trying to destroy in their drive for equal rights. The very young gay is similarly embarrassing because, to the general public, he is visible proof that homosexuals convert young boys to their way of life.

Both these stereotypes exist, of course, but to say they are typical of the homosexual life-style is nonsense. Public opinion, however, is rarely capricious and it's unlikely that it will change overnight. Responsible members of the gay community are aware of the problem of stereotyping and are taking steps to deal with it. It is difficult because there are, without a doubt, gay adults who are attracted to young boys. The difficulty is in differentiating between the boy who is gay and the boy who has the potential for becoming gay.

Morris Kight is the elder statesman of gay activists. He had been fighting for equal rights for homosexuals long before it became a fashionable cause. When he isn't traveling across the country to march, protest, demonstrate, or get someone out of jail, he runs a counseling program in Los Angeles for young gays and runaways. Kight angrily denounces professionals for prohibiting the organized gay community from playing an active role in the solution of the problem.

"Let me tell you what we think we know about these kids," he says. "The police and the bureaucrats who handle these welfare millions, and the officials who angrily tell us to do something about the parks and the beaches, the places where these kids congregate . . . if *they* would listen to us, it would be a miracle.

"If you want to know about the kids, start with the American family—the nuclear family: momma, poppa, and the kids. Gibran said, 'Your children are not your children' but in America kids are owned by momma and poppa and society. They teach, 'Consume-obey.' They tell their children, 'Take this dead hand of dead laws and sterile values and breathe some life into them.'

"The father becomes a figure of punishment and authority, and his oppressive hand is extended into all the institutions of society. He's the first to tell his son there's something wrong with him.

"At school, the boy gets his first encounter with authoritarian regimes. What do they teach him in those twelve dreary school years? 'Consume-obey,' forget aesthetic, self-expression, creativity, and humanity. Art is in the museums, not in the hand of man. The body and the senses—those are evil. And the teachers are merely baby-sitters who watch the kids while momma and poppa go to work, consuming and obeying.

"Every year there are millions of kids spewed out of our public schools who haven't learned a single skill and even if they have one, they can't get a job because we just don't have the jobs for them.

"Meantime, because the schools are teaching this blind obedience to authority, the kid also faces the enforced heterosexual training in the home. It's actually a form of rape. Either you become a heterosexual or your life is a disaster. The gangs that work the streets beating up gays think they have the sanction of society, and the tragedy is that they do. The lesson is clearly taught: Boys, prove your manhood. Girls, be feminine like momma. All signs of deviation from the pattern must be crushed.

"The churches are no better than the state . . . in fact, they're an extension of it. They teach power, revenge and blind obedience. 'God is going to punish you,' the boy is told. 'There's something wrong with me' he thinks to himself, long before he has the wherewithal to do anything which could be called a sin except in the most malevolent of imaginations.

"So 'repent' is added to 'consume-obey.' It's the erosion of the spirit.

"And when our politicians contrive to have a war, they order a boy to join in and tell him that God is on our side.

"The churches also offer this thing they call Holy Matrimony, but if you judge a relationship on the basis of tenderness and mutual respect, there are millions of mommas and poppas living in adultery and the boy can *see* that.

"For the chicanos, the Puerto Ricans, and the blacks, it's worse because they also learn this lethal thing they call "machismo," which simply alienates them further. The poor run away much sooner than the rich.

"Why don't families try to develop an atmosphere of creativity and love? Why don't they demand that the schools encourage pride and self-expression or be closed down so the billions can be spent on human institutions? Why don't they demand that the churches stop preaching this obedience and guilt? Why don't they stop making chattels of our children?

"Who wouldn't run away from an environment so alien to the human spirit? So they run away by the hundreds of thousands but, for many of them, it isn't long before they encounter the police arm of the state.

"For breaking curfew, or running away, or whatever, a boy will be taken into juvenile court where everything is contrived to be hostile even to the fact that he exists. Even a talk with a so-called counselor won't mean a thing when he's freezing in a cotton shirt.

"If the boy is gay, the social workers tell him to repent but in a far more subtle fashion. 'You're not sinful,' they'll assure him. 'We've got beyond all that. You're merely sick.'

"Is there any essential difference between the psychiatric industry and the old repressive churches? No ... but it's more lethal than the churches because it's got science on its side.

"So the boys find themselves in an environment of exploitation on both sides. The boy exploits the gays and the gays exploit him in return. Both parties are consumers, only this time it's the body that's up for sale. The older person gets the body in return for keeping it alive. If the boy is bright enough to see what's happening to him on the dead-end streets of hustling and drugs, where can he turn among the institutions of society? If he meets one of those religious fanatics who still work the streets, they'll take him upstairs to some kind of a 'temple' to 'save his soul' when what he needs is a job—which nobody has.

"A truly creative society would find millions of jobs by reclaiming this ravaged land of ours. Restore the deserts and the mountains; put up benches in the parks, where the weary soul can sit and rest for a while.

"But you want to know what's to be done about the problem of the boys in the street," Kight says. "Well, one of the first things that has to be done is to make social workers out of the police. Why can't a cop, when he finds a homeless boy on the streets, come up to him and say, 'I'm not going to arrest you for breaking curfew. I'm taking you to such-and-such a community center and I'm going to have you sprayed for lice, and then they're going to help you find a job. If you don't have the training for a job, I'm going to see that they enroll you in a school where you'll get that training.'

"What we also need in our cities is neighborhood courts where parents and real ministers and genuine social workers, and others who are really concerned about the boy will say to him: 'What are the positive things that we can build on? What are the things you like about yourself? What can we do to help?'

"Here at our center we've made a start. But the people in authority don't ask us what we need. We have to go to them, hat in hand, and beg for every dime while they demean us."

Kight takes a swing at America's role-models and says, "All of this is made so much more difficult by the cult of youth, which has been carried to such extremes by the advertising industry. Everyone in the ads is between eighteen and twenty years old with twenty-four-inch waists and Levis. All the products—from cars to clothes—are promises of youth.

"The boy who grows up in Ohio or Illinois is told 'Go West, young man.' Only the young can conquer. Don't bring the women and the men along. Don't let anybody with experience have anything to say.

"So the older men on the street believe that, above all else, they must get back their youth. How do they get it back? They buy it. They buy the boys and the boys give them youth. But there's no dignity in the transaction. It's not the loving teacher-learner relationsihp we know as Greek love.

" 'Hey, Pops,' says the boy. 'You wanna suck my cock?' And Pops himself rejects what he might teach the boy because he has rejected his own experience and years.

"So what is the boy waiting for when he hangs around the street? 'Somebody is going to buy me pretty clothes,' he thinks. 'Someone is going to put me in a car and take me to this luxury apartment in the Hollywood Hills.' Those are the values he was taught.

"My heart goes out to the families of these kids," says Kight. "They can't face the fact that their son might be gay because society teaches us there's nothing worse."

He continued, "Now it might be that even if we had the intake centers where we could rehabilitate the boy, he would say to us: 'Go to hell, man. I like peddling my ass.'

"When that happens—and it will if we don't find social workers who speak their language—then let's sit down with the boy and the police. Let's sit down and say to both of them: 'Can't we find a way to make this thing less violent? Do we have to have the beatings, the bustings, and the iron bars?' "

In New York, Bruce Voeller, Executive Director of the National Gay Task Force, makes a slightly different plea:

"Both American Society in general and many (not all) of the men who play parts in various aspects of boy prostitution are culpable. Too often, however, the man who likes boys bears the whole brunt of vehement recrimination . . . a scapegoat for our culture's guilt-ridden failings.

"At the National Gay Task Force, as at many of the nation's 1100 local gay organizations, we daily see the young victims of our nation's homophobia: On his high-school-graduation day one young sixteen-year-old gay youth from a small Pennsylvania town was given a one-way ticket to New York

City and put on the bus; his Baptist-minister father, in a familiarly Christian act, told him never to show his face there again, not even to *write* home. Three weeks later he stumbled into our offices, sick, starving and anguished. He'd slept in Central Park for several nights and then been discovered by a series of older men who fed him and had sex with him until he couldn't stand it any longer. Somehow someone in a gay bar sent him to us. We found him a job and a place to stay until he saved enough to rent his own apartment. Now he's thriving.

"Another young man didn't come to us until years later in his life, but he had a similar beginning. At fifteen he was beaten grievously by his father when his mother intercepted a love letter from another fifteen-year-old boy. His father threw him bodily out of the house and told him never to return. Al wandered from his Long Island town to Times Square, hustled his ass for three years, as much to find a little human warmth from another person as to earn survival dollars. One of these men discovered Al's remarkable musical talent and took him in. He helped him apply to, and work through, Juilliard. Al now is a successful flute player with one of the country's major symphonies and spends his spare time helping gay waifs.

"Yes, *some* of the men who hire boys are exploitive and vicious. But what about the parents who beat up their children and throw them into the street . . . parents more fearful of their neighbors' whisperings than loving of their own kids? What about the rabbis and ministers who preach hatred and venom toward young gays? What about the foster homes and juvenile institutions where young gays are raped and brutalized by their straight peers, and often the institution's wardens . . . where the gay kid who's raped or beaten is then labeled 'a problem child,' while his attackers are considered 'normal.' I frankly think that the older man who takes a kid in, even for sexual purposes, is a better alternative (woefully deficient as that is) for most kids than the horrors they come from: those

American homes and juvenile homes where they were so brutalized.

"But there is a third alternative which is a *real* solution when public hysteria can be blocked or avoided: *gay foster or adoptive parents for gay youth.* In New York City, we pioneered in battering down official resistance to placing gay teen-agers with gay foster parents. The fact that the service agencies considered gay youths to be 'problem children' provided us an excellent opportunity to persuade the agencies to solve their 'problem.' In all some thirty gay teen-agers were placed with gay parents. Similar projects have now begun in Washington, D.C., Minneapolis, and the states of Washington and California. All have been highly successful, by universal agreement.

"As an openly gay father, who has raised three heterosexual children (two boys and a girl), I myself know what a wonderful experience being a parent is. It is inexcusable in our society (or in any other society) with so many orphaned and estranged children to deprive adults or children from engaging in one of the great human experiences . . . sharing the love and education of one another in adult-child relationship.

"As the President of the American Psychiatric Association, Dr. John Spiegel wrote concerning gay teachers, 'I realize that many lay persons are concerned about the hiring of homosexuals as teachers. These concerns are the product of misunderstanding, not of scientific knowledge. Some, for instance, have feared that homosexual teachers might affect the sexual orientation of their students. There is no evidence to support this thesis, nor is there evidence to believe that seduction of a student by a homosexual teacher is any more likely to occur than heterosexual seduction.'

"The case is the same for gay parents."

To the police it's a problem of enforcement, or rather the inability to properly enforce it. Boy prostitution exists in every major city. The prostitutes are street hustlers who hang around in designated sections of town ready, willing, and able to do whatever must be done for the price. Usually, they're boys in their late teens or early twenties, waging a constant battle with the vice squad. Their field of operation and their methods parallel that of their female counterparts. The police operation against them is similar to that used against women hookers. Plainclothes vice officers hit the streets, playing the role of potential clients; a proposition is made, accepted, and then there's an arrest. But there the similarity ends.

New York Police Department's Sergeant William McCarthy and Captain Lawrence Hepburn explained it this way: "We can patrol an area where these kids are known to hang out. We can then watch what we know to be an obvious pickup. But from that point on our hands are tied. Let's assume, for example, that we decide to follow the adult and the child onto the subway and finally to the adult's apartment. . . . We have no legal reason to stop and question. Even if we do, in the hope of scaring them both off, we have no legal right to do so. When they arrive at the apartment and go in together, we have the same problem. If we want to break in on the assumption we'll catch them in a sex act, we first have to get a warrant. By the time we do that, the act—assuming there was one—has been completed."

McCarthy added, "We used to wait outside until the kid left the apartment alone, then we'd stop him and question him. I used to hope we could persuade the kid to set up a date with the adult at another time so we'd be ready to make an arrest, but the kids won't cooperate. They refuse to turn the guy in either because they like him, like what they're doing, or because they don't want to kill off the goose that's laying a golden egg."

Captain Hepburn agreed and added another element. "It's a strange situation," he said, "the way these kids will protect the adults. What makes it doubly strange is that the adults readily turn in one another. . . . Whenever we make an arrest, we end up with an indignant adult; indignant enough to tell us the names of other adults into the same thing without much prompting on our part."

Los Angeles's Sergeant Don Smith told a similar story: "If we make an arrest, and the boy and the adult have just met for the first time, it's relatively easy. But if the adult has been with the boy a couple of times previously and he's been nice to the boy, the boy clams up and protects him." For example, he said, "If the adult takes the boy to Disneyland or to a movie or fixes his bike, or anything that shows he's interested in the boy as well as his body, we're in real trouble because, in most cases like this, the boy is the only witness we've got."

At the time of the Houston murders, the Los Angeles Police Department, like many others, started checking their own backyards to see if there was any similar activity going on. LAPD found there was and there was an immediate flurry of arrests. At that time, LAPD had twenty-eight detectives assigned to the investigation of boy prostitution. As various leads developed, their investigations took them into nearly every state in the Union plus Canada and Mexico.

Deputy District Attorney James Grodin recounted that, at that time, he offered two options to then District Attorney Joseph Busch. First, be prepared to retain the twenty-eight detectives on a full-time basis and set up a new department to handle "chicken" cases exclusively. Also be prepared to go to court with the cases with the expectation of losing most of them. The second alternative was to discontinue the full-time investigation and handle cases as they'd been handled previously, on an individual basis. In the cases that were on the court docket at that time, it is significant that none of them had come to the attention of the police because of a parent complaint. Grodin recalled that during one case, the boy involved kept giving "thumbs-up" signs to his adult friend in the courtroom.

This "protection" of the adult by the boy bears out the supposition that many boys are becoming involved in acts of prostitution not so much for the money but for what they interpret as affection from the adult. The fact that they are prepared to enter into a sexual arrangement with an adult male—any adult male—to gain that affection would indicate a certain degree of desperation, of need. But one chickenhawk in Tucson, Arizona, maintains the boys are highly selective in their acceptance of a partner for an ongoing relationship. He claims, "There is a definite attraction for some of the local chickenhawks more than others.... Those who are physically unattractive or old have trouble finding boys even if they have plenty of money. There are other adults who are athletically inclined or drive fast sports cars or hunt or go to ball games—who do things the kids like to do—who have no trouble at all and I've known kids who literally fight with each other to get on certain guys' lists."

This attraction was summed up by a fourteen-year-old runaway from Long Island in an interview with *Newsweek*. Frankie told the reporter he had drifted to Times Square in New York and "before I knew what was happening" turned his first homosexual trick. The man took him home to an East Side penthouse, complete with burly leather furniture, deep furry rugs, and a flock of other chickens. Frankie moved in permanently. "I really didn't want to be on the streets," he explained. "It's so nice in the penthouse and there's always someone to talk to, older people as well as kids."

As we have seen, psychiatric opinions on the subject vary depending on the school of psychiatry or the individual opinion of the psychiatrist, but therapists with experience in the child-adult relationship seem to agree that such a homosexual encounter rarely has long-range consequences for the child. Dr. Martin Hoffman, Staff Psychiatrist at San Francisco's Center for Special Problems, said in a newspaper interview that the idea of childhood sexual trauma causing homosexual patterns to develop is a myth. He gave boarding-school life as an example in which, in spite of considerable homosexual activity, most students eventually marry and raise families.

When questioned about an incident in Santa Clara, California, where large numbers of teen-age boys had been involved in photographic and sexual sessions with a group of adults, Hoffman said he was not surprised; that some fathers are so concerned about their jobs and watching television that they do not give the attention to the children that they demand.

Hoffman told writer George Mendenhall that the adult who likes to "play with children" sexually is potentially headed for legal problems and the solution is that these adults seek therapy in which they may realistically face the problem. Mendenhall quotes Ron Lee, a gay activist and psychiatric social worker, as saying that adults who seek sexual activity with children have an inability to deal with adults in social-sexual situations. Lee says that such adults have difficulty in accepting their homosexuality, so they seem to relate better to straight children in a stage of exploration. "It is necessary that these people take a realistic assessment of what is demanded in our culture."

While these observations might well be correct, and are indeed confirmed by the life-styles of the boys on the streets, they are of little consolation to the parent suddenly faced with the glaring fact that his son has been involved in sexual activity with a male adult. In most cases, the parent's reaction is one of instant violence toward the boy. Due to inadequate sex education, the propagation of mythology, and a general distaste for homosexuals, the average parent overreacts. It is a very unusual parent who is capable of facing the problem with a "let's-sit-down-and-talk-this-out" attitude. Rather than seek professional help and advice, the average parent seeks professional police and punishment. An episode on television's "Doctor Marcus Welby" subscribed to this approach in 1975. A junior-high school student had been raped by his science teacher. The teacher, to protect himself, warned the boy that, if he was foolish enough to complain officially, all his buddies would think he was gay. The thrust of the program then dealt with the parents', and Welby's, concern that the boy had "lost his masculinity," when in fact, the only thing the show managed to prove was that the script's writer had lost his mind.

Parental concern about sexual attacks on their children, both male and female, is, of course, understandable. There is enough evidence from rape victims to indicate that the harrowing part of the experience is not the sexual attack itself (however harrowing that might be), but the judicial horrors that follow. The exposure, the questioning by police, the appearance in court, and the personal attacks by defense attorneys often leave the victim with mental scars that take years to heal, if ever.

One solution to this problem might be the establishment of crisis teams operating out of the neighborhood courts already suggested. Essentially, these teams would function in much the same way as the suicide-prevention hot lines, or the "help" lines already established in many cities. The crisis teams should consist of a social worker, a police officer, and possibly a minister. What they are is not nearly as important as what they would do. A family faced with a sex crisis; a rape, a molestation, or whatever (including family hassles over sex issues) could call for the team to provide instant face-to-face advice and direction. The team's function would be to speak to the family, either as a unit and/or individually. The police officer would have the authority to set the wheels in motion to arrest the rapist or the molester if that was indicated. In some cases it is possible the matter could be solved by the offender being confronted and directed to a treatment program. There is no indication that sex offenders have ever been successfully treated and cured by a long prison term. In the majority of cases that end up in court, a nominal defense invariably sets the culprit free on the streets again without any hope of treatment. He will, quite often, repeat his performance. If a man, confronted by the crisis team, faces the option of a court hearing or treatment, he would surely opt for the latter. Treatment at this point, rather than treatment ordered after a court hearing, would stand a far better chance of being successful.

A San Diego court is having trouble with the "castration or jail" option it offers to child molesters. In October, 1975, Superior Court Judge Douglas R. Woodworth angrily denounced members of the local medical profession because two child molesters would have to spend the rest of their lives in prison. They couldn't find a doctor to perform the *"humanitarian service"* of castrating them. Woodworth, saying he had no choice, sentenced the forty-five-year-old men to indefinite prison sentences. Said Woodworth during the sentencing of one of the men, "A whole branch of the medical profession has been unwilling to extend a humanitarian service to this man who faces the prospect of being locked in a cage for the rest of his life." Both men and their attorneys had spent months trying to find a surgeon to perform the operations. Most of the doctors refused, citing the possibility of malpractice suits and the fear that a court would rule that men facing the rest of their lives in prison could not truly give free consent to such an operation. Woodworth was unimpressed. "I sympathize with the doctors," he said, "but also with the human beings here who are seeking help."

*Chapter*

# 18

# The Homosexual Alternative

*"All human beings
are bisexual."*

It is not within the scope of this book to launch into a studied analysis of the phenomenon of homosexuality (if an act which has been practiced since the beginning of time can still be properly referred to as a phenomenon). In spite of the hundreds of books written on the subject and the thousands of studies undertaken, the causes and effects of homosexuality are still cloudy and debatable, with opinions ranging from those that claim an imbalanced chromosome count as responsible to those that think homosexuality a re-enactment of an ancient religious rite. For anyone who cares to take the time and make the effort to undertake an in-depth study, there are about two and a half tons of modern literature dealing with homosexuality, from the Kinsey Report to Dr. David R. Reuben's *Everything You Always Wanted to Know About Sex . . . But Were Afraid to Ask*, both of which were, and still are, challenged and denounced by opposing schools of thought.

Most of the books dealing with homosexuality were written by professionals for use by other professionals and make for very heavy reading. Even though some of the best minds in the country have addressed themselves to the problem, there is still no clear-cut answer to what causes homosexuality. In 1969, the National Institute of Mental Health appointed a Task Force on Homosexuality consisting of fifteen outstanding behavorial, medical, social, and legal scientists, each having extensive research and study experience in the areas of sexuality and sexual deviation. Their mandate was to review carefully the current state of knowledge regarding homosexuality and make recommendations for further study by the Institute. The Task Force was appointed by Dr. Stanley F. Yolles, Director of NIMH, and chaired by Dr. Evelyn Hooker, research psychologist at UCLA. When the study was completed, the Task Force recommended that all criminal laws dealing with homosexual acts be repealed while retaining legal sanctions against sexual behavior that violates public decency or involves the seduction of minors. It also recommended the removal of discrimination in employment of homosexuals. The members of the Task Force unanimously agreed that a Center for the Study of Sexual Behavior be established to further investigate the areas of research, training, education, prevention, and treatment.

But concerning the questions of social policy with respect to sexual behavior, three members of the Task Force issued minority reports claiming that there was a lack of reliable information.

Dr. Henry W. Riecken, President of the Social Science Research Council said: "In both the written papers and in the oral discussion of the Task Force there is an overpowering emphasis on our ignorance about the phenomenon of homosexuality and repeated mention of the paucity and inadequacy of the available data. Again and again, authors of the papers are forced to conjecture and to surmise, to estimate, or at best to rely on data from admittedly biased samples taken from an undefined population...."

"There is not even a clearly agreed upon definition of what a homosexual is, what a homosexual act is, or what homosexuality is apart from the rather bland assertion that it is deviant behavior. . . .

"The Task Force's own recommendations for increased research themselves emphasize and substantiate the extent of our ignorance. . . . It is as if they had said, 'Here is a phemonenon about which we know almost nothing, and about which there is a great deal of anxiety and concern; therefore, let us suggest a major revision in public policy for dealing with this phenomenon.' I cannot escape the belief that this is an utterly unreasonable conclusion to draw from the sea of ignorance and misinformation in which we find ourselves."

Dr. Clelland S. Ford, Professor of Anthropology at Yale University, added in a communication to the NIMH:

"While in essence I agree with Dr. Riecken's comments, I would state my view somewhat differently. I feel as he does that we do not have good scientific information about homosexuality, but more importantly we do not know enough about homosexuality in the context of our social life and culture and the function of the controls traditionally exercised over homosexual behavior to pass judgment upon them at this time. . . ."

Dr. Anthony F. C. Wallace, Professor of Anthropology, University of Pennsylvania, wrote to the NIMH:

"I have no problem in endorsing the two policy recommendations in themselves (i.e., that a homosexual act should not be regarded, in and of itself, as either a crime or cause for refusing employment). But I do so on the basis of personal moral conviction and not as the result of a review of the extremely, nay woefully, inadequate evidence. Thus I object, in effect, to dragging in the good name of science to give authority to a statement of policy recommendations which, in my opinion, do not spring from scientific research but from a mixture of common sense and 'liberal' social values.

"The matter appears important to me because it is becoming increasingly common for legislative, judicial, and administrative bodies to call upon the evidence of psychology, sociology, etc., to give the authority of 'science' to expressions of social value. This procedure is, in the long run, destructive of the credibility of science itself because it requires the scientist to claim that his findings are far more conclusive than in fact they are. My complaint about the Task Force report is that it implies that scientific research somehow backs up the policy statement when in fact all that really backs it up is moral conviction."

The need for caution suggested by the three minority reports has long been the hallmark of study groups. If you soberly profess not to have the answer, it lets you out of finding any, while issuing warnings not to move too rapidly avoids the necessity of getting started. The Hooker Report—as it was called—became an important document and played a major role in the 1974 decision by the American Psychiatric Association to rule that homosexuality should no longer be considered a sickness but should be categorized under the heading of "Sexual Orientation Disturbance."

Wardell Pomeroy, in his book *Dr. Kinsey and the Institute for Sex Research* indicates that Kinsey didn't suffer from such confusion regarding homosexuality. Says Pomeroy: "Kinsey had some specific advice to give to the homosexuals who wrote to him, and it flew in the face of both accepted psychological theory and psychoanalytic and psychiatric practice. But as he [Kinsey] liked to point out, no published study had a quarter as much material as he had on the subject. By the end of 1940 he had recorded more than 450 homosexual histories, enough to convince him that the psychologists were making matters worse by starting with the assumption that homosexuality was an inherited abnormality which could no be cured simply because it was inherent. Kinsey was convinced that there was absolutely no evidence of inheritance. The physical basis, he believed, of both homosexual and heterosexual behavior was a touch response. Whether an individual had a pleasurable first experience, of either kind, he looked forward to a repetition of the experience, often with such anticipation that he could be aroused by the light of another person with whom he might make contact. Unsatisfactory experience, on the other hand, built up a prejudice against repetition. Whether one built a heterosexual or homosexual pattern depended, therefore, partially on the satisfactory or unsatisfactory nature of one's first experience."

Kinsey also observed there were social factors too that forced an individual into a totally heterosexual or homosexual pattern. Most social forces encourage the former, but society's ostracism of the homosexual forces him into the exclusive company of other homosexuals and into an exclusively homosexual pattern. Without such social forces, Kinsey was convinced, many people would carry on both heterosexual and homosexual activities coincidentally.

The word for this coincidental duality is, of course, bisexuality, a condition that is becoming more and more acceptable to society. Gore Vidal, the eminent novelist who took a close look at the homosexual world in *The City and the Pillar* flatly states, "All human beings are bisexual," and adds that conditioning, opportunity and habit finally account for sexual preferences. Says Vidal: ". . . homosexualists are quite as difficult to generalize about as heterosexuals. They range from the transvestite who believes himself to be Bette Davis to the perfectly ordinary citizen who regards boys with the same uncomplicated lust that his brother regards girls."

More recently, Vidal attacked those who "cannot accept the following simple fact (certainly my own): that it is possible to have a mature sexual relationship with a woman on Monday, and a mature sexual relationship with a man on Tuesday, and perhaps on Wednesday have both together (admittedly you have to be in good condition for this)." Vidal made this statement in the *New York Review of Books*, June, 1970, while reviewing Dr. Reuben's book.

The vast majority of the boys described in this book are, indeed, technically bisexual: able to complete a sexual act with either a man or a woman. The majority of them eventually marry and raise families. The indications are that those who finally choose to accept the homosexual way of life would have done so even if they had not entered the field of prostitution.

Some psychiatrists take the position that all male prostitutes are homosexual, theorizing that if the boy is capable of being aroused by a homosexual act, achieving an erection, and reaching an orgasm, then he is, by definition, a homosexual. This belief indicates the single-mindedness that exists among each separate group of professionals trying to deal with the problem. The average boy hustler considers himself neither bisexual nor homosexual. He constantly insists he's "straight"; he's only performing homosexual acts for the money, and he really prefers girls. Indeed, in some societies (Italy, for example) it is common practice for a young man on the town to start his evening by selling himself to another man, thereby raising the necessary cash to later pay for the services of a female hooker. The operational differences between the male and female prostitute are most clearly defined by Paul H. Gebhard in an article in *Encyclopaedia Britannica 3*:

"In female prostitution the prostitute rarely or never reaches orgasm and the client almost invariably does; in male prostitution the prostitute almost invariably reaches orgasm, but the client frequently does not. This paradox is the result of a curious mythology, which the male hustler and his client feel compelled to enact. The homosexual male ideally seeks a masculine-appearing heterosexual male, and the prostitute attempts to fit this image. Consequently the prostitute can do little or nothing for or to the homosexual client lest he betray a homosexual inclination of his own and ruin the illusion. So the prostitute plays an essentially passive role and has orgasm (this is regarded as a necessary part of the bargain), while the client must ordinarily content himself with psychological arousal, self-masturbation, and body contact. This arrangement is reinforced by the male prostitute's protective image of himself as a 'real' and heterosexual man who tolerates homosexual activity solely for financial reasons. In actuality, of course, the hustler has a substantial homosexual component that is necessary or he could not achieve erection and orgasm; and many of them are predominantly homosexual in orientation, though loath to admit it. One might regard this as the reverse of female prostitution: the female stimulates a passion she does not feel, whereas the male prostitute conceals a passion he does feel." Gebhard adds: "There is some evidence that this curious pattern of feigned indifference is gradually breaking down and that more male prostitutes are taking an active role in the sexual relation while maintaining a masculine image."

The homosexual community has adopted several phrases to describe its life-style. They include "gay pride," "gay awareness," "gay consciousness," and "the homosexual alternative." The first three are self-explanatory and quite possibly self-serving. The fourth, "the homosexual alternative, implies a choice of life-style which may be selected or rejected at will. It is a matter of considerable debate whether there is a choice to be made. Some clinicians say there is none; that the die has been cast by the time one reaches one's seventh birthday. This suggestion is currently popular, but it is based on the premise that a person must be either a homosexual or a heterosexual. The theory ignores the concept of bisexuality or denounces it completely. However, this just doesn't square with the facts. Even if it did and there was a choice of life-style, the homosexual alternative is not the best choice.

The countless self-deceptions which take place in every phase of American life may well be necessary prerequisites for survival in a fragmented and polarized society. But to choose the homosexual life-style is to compound instantly the necessity for self-deception. The homosexual adopts and lives a double life and has to function in two separate worlds, each with a different set of standards. In his straight life, he constantly has to play a role—always with the underlying fear of discovery, the sudden hostility of straight friends and neighbors, and even the loss of his job.

To the young boy who slowly realizes that he's sexually attracted to other boys, the homosexual alternative is a triple-horror. It isn't an occasion for celebration. He doesn't think, "I now have an opportunity to choose the homosexual alternative." He relates his sexuality to "fag," "queer," "fruit," "pervert," . . . all the terms he's heard at home or on the street. And that's a mind-bending realization for a teen-ager or a pre-teen. More often than not, there is no one to turn to for advice; no one to confide in. A tentative, shy pass made at a school buddy could turn into a disaster if it is interpreted correctly—and rejected.

*Chapter*

# 19

# The Extent
# of the Problem

*"The* majority *of Boy Scouts
get along quite well."*

 

A book of this nature requires the assembly of a tremendous amount of data and case histories. When it's all put together and the final package read as a whole, it is inevitable that the reader will be left with the general impression that the majority of young boys are hustling and that a vast army of older men are prowling the streets in search of them.

Nothing could be further from the truth. The boys in this book represent a small minority within a minority. There is no evidence to indicate that boy prostitution is on the increase. What is on the increase is the availability of data that denotes its existence and the open discussion of this formerly hidden activity.

The *majority* of Boy Scouts get along quite well, absorbed in the intricacies of a bowline-on-a-bight rather than anal intercourse.

The *majority* of Big Brothers manage to limit their activities with their Little Brothers to camping, hiking, bowling, and other wholesome occupations.

The *majority* of boys hitchhiking get to where they intend to go without any stopovers at strange apartments.

And the *majority* of boys grow up without even knowing that some of their peers are hustling.

An important question remains: how many boy prostitutes are there? Truthfully, nobody knows. There would be no way of knowing and no accurate way of finding out. But there are enough known statistics in related areas to enable one to arrive at a reasonable conclusion. There are one million runaways wandering around the country each and every year. As you have read, a large majority of the young hustlers are drawn from this army. Another indicator is the sale of a book *Where the Young Ones Are*, a guide to amusement parks, hamburger stands, beaches, and street corners across the country where young boys are said to be available. Whether the book is accurate or not is academic. What is important is that it sold 70,000 copies at five dollars apiece.

Throughout the book there are references to the hundreds of so-called "chicken" magazines and to the several hundred photographs in them. But don't fall into the trap of taking these figures and totaling them on an adding machine because there are obvious duplications and triplications. For example, many of the pictures of boys in sex acts found during the Houston raid would appear in more than one magazine. Twenty pornographic films taken in a raid might mean that ten prints of two different films were seized. But with such a tremendous market in chicken literature, chicken films, and chicken photographs, there is obviously a great number of buyers keenly interested in kids.

In the early stages of research for this book, I approached police officers and leaders of the gay community with a working figure of 300,000 boy prostitutes. Deputy District Attorney James Grodin, in Los Angeles said, "You won't get any argument from this office on that figure." During a television interview, I offered the same figure to Morris Kight, the West Coast gay activist, who said: "It might well be double that amount."

But both Kight and Grodin were agreeing to what was—at its best—a gut hunch. Indeed, the only absolutely accurate figure I can personally guarantee is a head-count made in New York on a cold Sunday afternoon in two amusement arcades near Times Square. I was accompanied by a guide who knew the boys working that particular section of town, and we counted seventy-five boys, under sixteen years of age, in a period of one hour, with no duplications. There are, of course, the boys involved in the Boise, Idaho, and Waukesha, Wisconsin, scandals and in other police raids. These are known figures. There are also the statements from the boys themselves. Each boy I interviewed knew at least five or six others gainfully employed in the same business, excluding kids who hustle part-time after school, on weekends, or on holidays. There's also the "occasional" hustler, the boy who hustles for a specific reason, perhaps to buy a present for Mother's Day or for his girl's birthday, to pay off a parking ticket or buy a new transmission for his car. For the active chicken hawk, these boys are prime material not only for sex but for referrals to others. If a man is looking for a fourteen-year-old boy, the best way to make contact is to ask a sixteen-year-old boy. He will surely know someone younger—quite often, his brother.

The key, I think, to the question of how many boys are active prostitutes lies not so much in how many there presently are, but in how many are becoming potentially available through circumstances beyond their control.

You have read how many children are being incarcerated in "corrective" institutions and what happens to them while they're there. You have read about the familial conditions that send a million kids fleeing from their home towns to unknown destinies elsewhere. You have read what happens when these same kids run into the arms of the law and are injected into the juvenile-justice system for their "protection and best interests." If, after reading that, you are still not quite convinced that this particular sub-rosa culture exists as America's best-kept secret, then there are several hundred people you could approach directly; people who know about it; people who work with it on a daily basis; people who will be more than happy to tell you about it because the greatest frustration in their life is getting people to listen . . . and to act.

You could ask Patrick Keenan, an Assistant Professor at the DePaul University College of Law in Chicago. He was appointed, by the Illinois Department of Children and Family Services (IDCFS), to investigate privately-owned children's homes in Texas. The probe was ordered by Dr. Jerome Miller, who was then the director of IDCFS—the same Jerome Miller who had previously brought about massive juvenile reform in Massachusetts.

Close to a thousand dependent and neglected children (known as D & N's) had been placed in Texas homes by the state of Illinois. But Illinois had neither monitored the children while they were in Texas reformatories, nor exerted any continuing control over their care. On the rare occasions when an Illinois official traveled to Texas to inspect the various facilities, he would be carefully wined and dined and handed a smooth line of double-talk by the operators of the homes. As an inevitable consequence, reports were written that told of the adequate care and overall well-being of the children.

Although at the time of Keenan's probe Illinois had poured over $8,000,000 into the Texas homes, the introduction to his report was entitled "An Illinois Tragedy." In an interview, Keenan said he found all the children educationally deprived; all had suffered violations of their legal rights; and "many had sustained permanent injuries and will wear life-long scars on their bodies or spirits. At least three children had died and a great number had just literally been placed in storage."

Keenan added that while a few shrewd Texans had profited greatly, in Illinois "poor administrative practices, atrocious record-keeping, and excessive paperwork" had prevented workers from being sensitive to the needs of the children and aware of the conditions in which they existed. Former top administrators were strongly criticized for failure to "exercise their purchasing muscle" in persuading private agencies in Illinois to care for the state's children. Keenan called Illinois "a mindless, heartless, bureaucratic monster" for sending children to Texas and using Texas homes as "warehouses for Illinois human baggage." The report itself is a grim document of nearly 200 pages that equates "treatments" and practices in the Texas homes with those in prison camps. Jerome Miller made the report public and ordered the children returned to Illinois.

A number of schools, taking in twenty-five dollars a day per Illinois child, solved their overcrowding problem in an ingenious way. As a new group of kids arrived at the home, a like number was sent into the wilderness on "camping trips." At the three Wimberley Schools located near San Antonio, children were sent on these camping trips for as long as eighteen months. The children did not stay in any permanent structure for more than a couple of weeks and did not attend public school. The forests and fields were used as low-cost holding areas. Keenan estimated that children living in tents and using thin sleeping bags required only 25 percent of the money Illinois had made available for their care. A former consultant for the Wimberley Schools said he had asked for the purchase of better camping equipment, including sleeping bags, since temperature would often fall below the freezing point. The price of the equipment was considered. The request was turned down.

The Keenan report lists many horrendous episodes in which professional workers acted in "the best interests of the child." The following are just examples:

Joseph D. Farrar, the Director of Artesia Hall in Houston and a self-proclaimed but unlicensed doctor, has been charged with the alleged murder of a seventeen-year-old girl. The indictment claims she was denied medical care after poisoning herself.

Brother Roloff, operator of Brother Roloff Evangelical Enterprises, deals with long hair by pulling it out by the roots.

A worker at the East Texas Guidance and Achievement Center described beatings in which a four-foot piece of white ash was used. It was half an inch thick and three inches wide. In this impressively named institution the sewer system backs up and keeps the corridors flooded with water and waste; the roof leaks so badly that at night, when it's raining, the boys have to move their beds to avoid the downpour. The children were described as being dressed in rags.

At another school, a child being subjected to a form of punishment called "state confinement" would be attached to a staff member by a five-foot length of rope, permitted to wear only pajamas, and had to go everywhere the staff member went and do everything he did. School officials asserted the punishment was psychologically beneficial since the rope "symbolized the umbilical cord."

Elsewhere in Texas, boys who had attempted to run away were placed in front of an assembly of other inmates, and each was given two injections: one of alcohol, one of Thorazine. The reason given for the shot of alcohol was "to make it sting." Keenan says: "The numbing litany could go on for volumes."

In considering the $8,000,000 laid out by Illinois taxpayers, Keenan says, "The highest cost and the most tragic loss is borne by the children who were sent to Texas. Everyone who suffered physical discomfort or abuse in the guise of 'getting treatment' sustained injuries which are difficult to price and for which there is probably no remedy." He adds: "The normal children on whom 'treatment' was practiced have suffered an incalculable loss; there are cases of children who received unneeded or experimental drugs . . . the aggregate human cost is staggering."

In the conclusion of his report Keenan states: "At the inception of the investigation, everyone hoped and preferred to believe that the Texas rip off was just that . . . a criminal conspiracy of a few evil people making and taking interstate bribes. It would have been so much simpler and infinitely easier to remedy. Alas, the worst fears were realized. Everyone is responsible. No one is, or will be, accountable. No one meant it to happen. It just did. But if the mutilation of a child's spirit is indeed the most deadly of sins, let us confess and learn from the Texas mistake. . . ."

You could ask Ken Wooden about the sub-rosa culture. Wooden is now looking into child-care arrangements in New Jersey and Louisiana. Supported by foundation grants, he spends his life investigating both private and public institutions. He is the Ralph Nader of the booming kid business and says, "I'm going after the child-care industry that perpetuates itself, provides jobs and political clout. I'm going after those institutions that give the illusion of treatment but abuse children and make big, big money."

When it comes to mistreatment, Wooden has first-hand experience. As a child he was diagnosed as mentally retarded, branded as incorrigible, and flunked out of school after being encouraged to fail. It was Wooden who was responsible for publicly revealing that in Orange City, Florida, at the Green Valley School, emotionally disturbed and delinquent children were being injected with their own urine. The children were told they were "morally dead," forced to dig graves and lie in them overnight, shackled and tortured with an electric-shock machine called a "lalapalooza," and given loaded guns and told to commit suicide. The school, supported by 1.2 million dollars of the taxpayers' money was, like 486 other schools around the country, for dependent children of U.S. military personnel. When Wooden took his findings to the United States Senate,

Senator Henry Jackson referred to Green Valley as an institution worthy of "Hitler, Ilse Koch, and Buchenwald." Indeed, some of the same Texas children's homes exposed by Keenan were part of the network of institutions funded by the Civilian Health and Medical Program of the Uniformed Services (CHAMPUS), which will match the highest rate paid to a home by a private client, and has laid out as much as seventy-five dollars per day per child—not counting the high additional costs of psychiatric care. CHAMPUS has spent up to 100 million dollars a year for psychiatric care, the quality of which is questionable.

Wooden found homosexual activity in many of the schools he visited, while Keenan recounts all forms of sexual abuses in the Texas schools, including one in which a worker would lock two naked children in a room together to "observe" them. The only equipment in the room was a bed and a selection of pornographic magazines.

You could, if it were possible, talk to the young boy in a county detention center in the southwest who scratched on the glass of his solitary-confinement cell: "As you are, I was once. As I am, you shall be." Then he hanged himself. . . .

Or you could ask any street-boy, because they're around and available in any major city.

I found one in particular at seven-thirty in the morning on Forty-Second Street just around the corner from Times Square, in New York. There's not much going on in Times Square at that hour of the day. The streets, freshly scrubbed by a hissing, clanking, mechanical monster were nearly deserted that May morning. The canyons were yawning themselves awake to the padded thrum of tires as the city—reluctantly—started to come alive. The tourists were still asleep and the stores, not yet ready for them, were still protected from the night prowlers by

sliding steel bars. I had arrived from California the night before. Later that day I would meet in this same area with New
York police officers and members of the gay community, and I
wanted to make an early appraisal of the area we would walk
through.

I heard the footsteps of someone behind me, sliding up from
out of nowhere; a boy about twelve years old, maybe five feet
tall, neatly dressed in a pair of double-knit pants and an electric-
blue Windbreaker. A bright orange, wool ski cap was cocked
jauntily over one eye. With a swift appraising glance and an
engaging smile, he asked what time it was. There was a number
of digital clocks flashing away on the tops of the buildings. I
glanced at one of them and read off the time. He grinned and
explained, "I was just seeing whether you were a cop."

Through that sixth sense that street-people acquire, the
boy decided he wasn't in any danger and fell in step beside me.
Completely at ease, chattering incessantly, he moved like a
young boxer, spinning around and throwing punches as we
talked about the karate movies we were passing. His 100-pound
frame would rocket in and out of doorways as he tried to im-
press me with his agility and toughness. Between fights he
offered some information that his home was "uptown" and that
he had spent the night with a friend who lived "downtown."

After sending a crumpled Dixie cup flying with a well-
placed kick, he said, almost casually, "Do you want to fool
around for a while?"

"How do you mean . . . fool around?" I asked.

He smiled. "Aren't you looking for a young guy to fool
around with?"

I was cautious. "It depends. What do you do and what's it
going to cost?"

He took another swipe at some sidewalk litter and said,
"Between ten and fifteen bucks . . . depending."

"Depending on what?" I queried.

He spun around, squared off in front of me, and said defiantly, "For fifteen bucks I do everything."

The transformation was almost magical. At that precise moment he changed from a little boy into a small, street-hardened adult; a little person.

I changed the subject. "What I want right now is breakfast. How about you?" At one of the ham 'n egg joints that punctuate midtown Manhattan, he rattled off stories about himself as he wolfed down an amazing amount of food. On the first round he said his father owned two heavy construction companies. Life at home was a good life and when he graduated from school—where he was doing "pretty well"—he would go into business with his father.

As he continued to talk, his facts began to contradict themselves and amendment followed amendment. In the final version, his father didn't own a construction company. He drove a truck for a construction company. The boy himself wasn't doing "pretty well" in school; in fact he had dropped out six months previously. Life at home wasn't even good enough to want to be there. It was a drag; one big, nagging hassle. He had not spent the night with a friend but with a client. When the client went off to work, the boy had been put out on the street again.

He was, in a way, slightly embarrassed by having to change his story so many times ". . . what with you buying my breakfast and everything." But he desperately enjoyed talking. He needed to talk—to anyone—about anything. A female prostitute would, by this time, have demanded some firm commitment so she could get back on the street to turn another trick. The boy insisted he hustled only when there were no other jobs to be had. In defense of his masculinity he reeled off a list of girl friends and a vivid description of their sexual prowess. As I paid the check and we left, he re-emphasized that, when he worked, he always played the masculine role. He jerked a thumb in the direction of his rear end and said sternly, "I don't go for anything back there." When he found I wasn't interested in his body, he was almost relieved and scurried off down the street. As he left, it occurred to me that I didn't even know his name.

I saw him on the street many times over the next two weeks. He'd always wave eagerly and charge across the street, weaving in and out of the traffic like a rabbit, to "borrow" a dollar to go to a movie.

On my last day in New York, a cold, blustery Sunday afternoon, I was standing on Forty-Second Street with a chicken hawk who knew every juvenile hustler on the street. He had scored with most of them at one time or another. Standing across the street from Playland, we watched the kids cavorting with the constant parade of adults going in and out of the amusement arcade. As they played the machines, they watched the kids—and the kids knew they were being watched. My guide nudged me and whispered through the din of traffic that someone was about to make a pickup.

Next to Playland, a gaunt man in his sixties who looked like a mortician was talking to a boy who, his back towards us, was gazing intently into a store window. While they negotiated, my guide said, "I know that boy. I made it with him once . . . but never again because he embarrassed me."

I said, "How do you mean . . . he embarrassed you? You mean he told someone about you?"

"No," he replied. ". . . it wasn't that. He was recommended by another young friend of mine—Steve. And Steve was right about one thing. That kid does everything in bed . . . and I mean everything. But while he was lying there, and I was doing all the work, I heard this strange whimpering sound like a lost puppy. I looked up and his eyes were closed tight. He was sucking his thumb like a baby and making this whimpering sound. It completely turned me off and left me with such a guilty feeling I didn't come down to the street for three days."

As he finished the story, the transaction across the street was completed and the man and boy hurried through the rain toward the subway station. As they turned, I saw the face of the boy I had met on my first day in New York. He didn't see me.

My guide sniffed. "If you want to interview him, I suppose I could arrange it. His name's Jimmy. He's from West Virginia."

> "Someday, maybe, there will exist a well-informed, well-considered, and yet fervent public conviction that the most deadly of all possible sins is the mutilation of a child's spirit; for such mutilation undercuts the life principle of trust, without which every human act, may it feel ever so good, and seem ever so right, is prone to perversion by destructive forms of consciousness."
>
> —ERIK ERIKSON

# For Money or Love
## Boy Prostitution in America
### BY Robin Lloyd
### Introduction by Senator Birch Bayh

Boy Prostitution. A subject most people don't talk about—or if they do, it's only with revulsion. And yet this is a problem of major proportions: perhaps 300,000 boys, aged 8 to 17 (chickens), are selling themselves to male adults (chickenhawks) throughout the country every day. Who are these boys? What kind of lives do they lead? And what about the chickenhawks: Who are they, why do they find it necessary to procure young boys for sexual fulfillment?

FOR MONEY OR LOVE reveals, for the first time, how young boys enter the sub rosa culture of prostitution and how they operate once they get there. It explores the various types of chickens: those who are looking for money, and those who are looking for love; those who work the streets, and those who seek longer-lasting relationships. It crosses the country—from New York to Los Angeles, Waukesha, Wisconsin, to Dallas, Texas—probing the extent of the problem and showing that no town, no matter how small, is permanently immune from a scandal related to boy prostitution.

In the process, FOR MONEY OR LOVE attempts to get to the "roots of alienation," which are wide ranging and deep: the school system, parental upbringing, and a host of other socio-economic forces. But this book is not a sociological study. It is an investigative exposé by an award-winning journalist.

*Reader take note:* this book may offend—there is sex and perversion, people who don't give a damn and who are out to make a fast buck. But there are others who *do* care, who want to resolve the problem of boy prostitution—including the author himself, who brings to light with substance and understanding a subject dealt with previously in book form only in pornography.